NORTH CYPRUS

A COMPLETE GUIDE

(Illustrated, with maps and plans)

Rainer Schmidt

Brian Worley Jnr.

Pilot Publications

London

1992

First published by Pilot Publications in 1991

Revised edition published in 1992

ISBN 0-9517705-1-9

Printed and bound in the Turkish Republic of Northern Cyprus by

Tezel Offset Printing Co. Ltd.

Lefkoşa

CONTENTS

Contents

Contents

Contents

INTRODUCTION

In Cyprus are combined a number of features within a compact area which makes the island worth including on a short list of holiday venues.

Cyprus is at present a divided island, and this book addresses the Northern sector which is well endowed with archaeological and historical sites as well as places of natural beauty; and of course, visitors from colder northern climes may realize their office reveries of warm sandy beaches sloping down to the sunlit sea.

Beaches, however, do not require explanations: the visitor will enjoy them without instruction. On the other hand, archaeological and historical sites, whilst they can be superficially appreciated by the lay person, acquire much more interest when accompanied by a little background information.

For centuries Cyprus has been a choice morsel snatched up by the major powers prevailing in the eastern Mediterranean, and this fate has resulted in the rich mosaic of cultural influences which colour Cypriot tradition and culture today. An attempt has been made in this book to place sites of interest into an historical context, and an extensive historical survey has been included in the hope that the reader will gain some feeling of continuity in the ebb and flow of civilization on the island.

A hire car is recommended for the visitor who wishes to explore Northern Cyprus. (Further information on this and other subjects may be found in the chapter entitled General Information, at the back of this book) The visitor should not hesitate to turn off the beaten track: a couple of hours spent with the hospitable and friendly locals in a remote village coffeeshop may well be the event which remains in the memory long after the monuments have faded into a blur of rubble.

The best months of the year to visit Cyprus are from March to June, and from September to November, although hardcore sun specialists may enjoy the challenge of July and August.

The place names used in this guide are the post 1974 Turkish names, which are seen on road signs, except for Kyrenia, Nicosia, and Famagusta, which are internationally known in their anglicised form. For reference purposes, the Greek names are shown in parentheses.

1

MYTHOLOGY

According to mythology, Cyprus is the island of Aphrodite, that enigmatic goddess of love.

Her birth from the waves, a favourite theme of European artists, was described by the poet Hesiod in his *Theogeny*, written in the 8th century BC. In the beginning, he writes, there was chaos, and from this chaos there appeared Gaea, the deep breasted earth. Gaea bore Uranus, the sky, *'whom she made her equal in grandeur, so that he entirely covered her'*. Gaea and Uranus united, producing first the Titans, six male and six female, then the Cyclopes, with their single eye set in their foreheads, and lastly three monsters. Uranus condemned his offspring to captivity in the bowels of the earth, but a sad, and then angry Gaea planned her revenge. Her son and confederate, Cronus (one of the Titans) lay in wait until his father fell asleep at Gaea's side one night. He then drew forth a steel sickle, fashioned by his mother and mutilated Uranus, casting the bleeding genitals into the sea. The severed organs broke into a white foam from which arose the beautiful young goddess Aphrodite, *'who was first carried towards the divine Cythera and thence as far as Cyprus surrounded by waves'*, where she landed at sandy Paphos. Here she was met by the Horae, or Seasons, dressed in precious garments, and conducted to the assembly of the gods.

Mythologists, who regard myths as a reflection of social and historical events and conflicts, have devised the following sequence to account for this story: Gaea, the mother earth, who came into being without male assistance, represents a matriarchal society existing in prehistoric times. In contrast, Aphrodite came into existence from the male organ alone, with no role for the mother, and this has been held to represent a patriarchal society. Thus this myth is supposed to signify the change from a matriarchal to a patriarchal society.

Aphrodite is the essence of female seductive beauty and the object of male desire. Hesiod attributes her with *'gracious laughter, sweet deceits, the charms and delights of love'*. She is often accompanied by Eros, with his bow and quiver full of passion tipped arrows, and Himeros, the personification of tender desire.

Ironically, the ill favoured Hephaestus, god of the forge, obtained Aphrodite for his wife, but the goddess of love did not lack amorous adventure. In the Odyssey, Homer tells of her affair with Ares, the god of war: the lovers eagerly took advantage of Hephaestus' absence, but the infidelity of his wife was reported to him by Helios, who sees all. In response, Hephaestus forged a net invisibly fine, yet unbreakably strong, and contrived to ensnare the couple as they slept on his couch. He then called on Zeus and the Immortals to witness their adultery, and the sight of helpless couple inspired the gods to Olympian laughter, throwing the awakening Ares and Aphrodite into the utmost confusion.

The connection between Aphrodite and Hephaestus is of particular significance to Cyprus, bearing in mind the importance of copper, and copper working, to the island. Excavations by archaeologists at the city of Enkomi showed that the forges where copper was worked were associated with temple complexes. Furthermore, a male and a naked female statuette were found, each standing on an ingot of copper.

The myths in which Aphrodite features are many, and her emergence as a cult figure in Cyprus has been connected to the story of Pygmalion. This sculptor, sometimes referred to as the King of Amathus, carved such a captivating female image in ivory, that he fell in love with it. Aphrodite took pity on Pygmalion as he caressed the curves of his inert creation, and breathed life into the statue, which began to return the sculptors ardour.

The union of Pygmalion and Galataea - so named on account of her milk white skin - produced Paphos, whose son Kinyras founded the city of Paphos where he raised a temple to Aphrodite renowned in ancient times.

Metharme, the wife of the priest-king Kinyras, foolishly boasted that her daughter Myrrha (Smyrna) excelled Aphrodite in beauty. The scorned goddess retaliated by inspiring in Myrrha a lust for her father. One night, when Kinyras was in his cups, an incestuous union took place. However, when Kinyras discovered that he was both father and grandfather to his daughter's unborn child, he sought to hunt and slay her. Aphrodite saved Myrrha from his fury by transforming her into a myrtle tree which some months later bore her son Adonis.

Aphrodite fell for the comely youth, and concealed him from rivals in a chest which she entrusted to Persephone, the goddess of the underworld. Persephone could not resist opening the chest, and, captivated by its contents, she took Adonis as her lover. Aphrodite appealed to Zeus against this perfidy, and he passed the problem on to the Muse, Caliope. She judged that Adonis should spend one third of the year with Aphrodite, one third with Persephone, and the remaining third alone, to recover from his exertions.

According to another version, Adonis was fatally gored by a wild boar. From his blood sprang the wild anemones, and from Aphrodite's tears, the rock roses which carpet the fields of Cyprus late each Winter.

This symbolism has suggested the identity of Adonis with Tammuz, the oriental god of vegetation, whose spouse was Astarte, the Phoenician fertility goddess. The conclusion that Aphrodite herself is a transformation of Astarte - the Phoenicians were early colonisers of Cyprus - was mooted long ago by Herodotus. It is clear that in prehistoric times, gods acquired aspects according to the movements of and the interaction between, the various races in the region. No doubt the primitive female fertility idols found in Neolithic sites in Cyprus were the pegs on which the developing features of the goddess were hung.

Whatever her origin, Aphrodite became a potent goddess in Cyprus, and her temple in Paphos was famous throughout the Mediterranean basin at least as far back as Homeric times, and attracted pilgrims up until the 4th century AD.

Chronological Table

Stone Age:		
Neolithic I	7000 - 6000 BC	
Neolithic II	4500 - 3900 BC	
Chalcolithic	3900 - 2600 BC	

Bronze Age:		
Early Bronze Age	2300 - 1850 BC	
Middle Bronze Age	1900 - 1600 BC	
Late Bronze Age	1650 - 1050 BC	

Iron Age:		
Geometric Period	1050 - 750 BC	
Archaic Period	750 - 475 BC	
Classical Period	475 - 325 BC	

Hellenistic Period	325 - 58 BC
Roman Period	58 BC - 330 AD
Byzantine Period	330 - 1191
Frankish Period (Lusignans)	1192 - 1489
Venetian Period	1489 - 1571
Ottoman Era	1571 - 1878
British Rule	1878 - 1960
Republic of Cyprus	1960 -
T.R.N.C.	1983 -

Lusignan Monarchs of Cyprus

Amaury obtained a crown from the Holy Roman Emperor, Henry IV, and thus became the first King of Cyprus in 1197. From 1269, the monarch was known as the King of Jerusalem and Cyprus, and from 1368, as King of Jerusalem, Cyprus and Armenia.

1192-94	Guy de Lusignan	* Sibylla of Jerusalem
1194-1205	Amaury (brother)	* Echive d'Ibelin
		* Isabel of Jerusalem
1205-18	Hugh I (son)	* Alice de Champagne
1218-53	Henry I (son)	* Alice de Montferrat (1229)
		* Stephania (1237)
		* Plaisance of Antioch (1250)
1253-67	Hugh II (son)	
1267-84	Hugh III (cousin)	* Isabel d'Ibelin
1284-85	John I (son)	
1285-1324	Henry II (brother)	* Constance of Aragon
1324-59	Henry IV (nephew)	* Marie d'Ibelin
		* Alix d'Ibelin
1359-69	Peter I (son)	* Echive de Montfort (1342)
		* Eleanor of Aragon (1353)
1369-82	Peter II (son)	* Valentina Visconti (1372)
1382-98	James I (uncle)	* Heloise de Brunswick-Grubenhagen
1398-1432	Janus (son)	* Heloise Louise Visconti (1372)
		* Charlotte de Bourbon
1432-58	John II (son)	* Medea de Montferrat (1440)
		* Helena Palaeologina (1441)
1458-60	Carlotta (daughter)	* Louis of Savoy (1458)
1460-73	James II (half-brother)	* Caterina Cornaro (1472)
1473-74	James III (son)	
1474-89	Caterina Cornaro	

HISTORICAL SURVEY

Neolithic (7000 - 3900 BC)

The earliest traces of settlement in Cyprus go back to the 7th millenium BC. Mesolithic and Paleolithic remains have not been discovered, but may yet exist. The origin of the first settlers is unclear, but there are archaeological links with sites on the mainland to the north and east.

Extensive excavations at Khirokitia in the south of the island have revealed evidence of two cultural phases, pre-pottery Neolithic I (7000 - 6000 BC), and Neolithic II (4500 - 3900 BC), associated with *combed ware* pottery. The circular dwellings *(tholoi)* at Khirokitia were made with massive stone and mudbrick walls, with a domed mudbrick roof.

An important settlement from the second period was found on the north coast, east of Kyrenia, known as Ayios Epiktitos Vrysi. The houses were half-sunk and roofed with wood and thatch. Narrow covered passages linked the houses. Amongst the finds unearthed were polished stone axes and chisels, and stone idols, whose abstract forms strike a chord with those observers familiar with modern art. This period also sees the first appearance of *red on white ware*, a reddish brown coating on white ceramic, frequently decorated with lines and dots in reserved white areas. Combed ware is less common. The style of pottery here and at Troulli, 3 miles further to the east, refers to traditions found on the mainland at Mersin. Obsidian finds at both sites also point to an Anatolian connection.

Little light has been shed on the gulf between Neolithic I & II: the island may have been temporarily abandoned on account of a natural catastrophe, or perhaps intermediate sites have not yet been recognised.

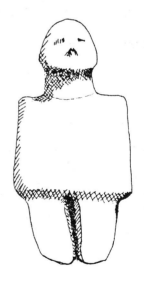

STATUETTE MADE OF
ANDESITE

Chalcolithic (3900 - 2600 BC)

This period marks the first introduction of copper tools, which were probably imported from the Anatolian mainland. Local manufacture may have been pursued at this time, but no evidence of dross from the smelting process has been uncovered.

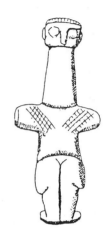

The round house style of the Neolithic period continued to be used, but the dead were no longer buried under the houses, but in cemeteries outside the village.

Red on white pottery was more skilfully executed, and towards the end of the period, a standardised type of ceramic appeared on the island, similar

CROSS SHAPED IDOL.

to that found in Early Bronze Age layers in Tarsus on the Cilician coast.

Cross shaped soapstone idols which were placed in graves or worn around the neck as talismans are characteristic of the Chalcolithic era. At this time a cult of the dead arose, associated with rites centred on a female fertility symbol.

Early Bronze Age (2300 - 1850 BC)

During the Early Bronze Age the first towns and economic centres developed in Cyprus where copper was worked and exported. At this time the island developed commercial and cultural relations with Asia Minor, Egypt, and the Syrian/Palestinian region. This fresh impulse resulted from an influx of immigrants from Anatolia who were displaced from their settlements in Asia Minor by invading tribes. The newcomers brought with them, along with their customs, a shiny dark red type of pottery, known as *red polished ware.*

The dead were interred in rock cut tombs accessed by long narrow passages. Most of our knowledge of this period is derived from finds in cemeteries, for although the island seems to have been thickly populated at this time, no settlements have yet been identified. Judging by the multitude of articles placed with the dead - bowls, jugs, food, combs, knives, necklaces, spinnings whorls etc. - the afterlife was evidently an important cultural feature of these Bronze Age people.

A clay model found in Vounous showed the existence of enclosed areas, or *temenoi*, which served as sanctuaries. This model, representing a religious ceremony, centres on three symbolic figures wearing bull masks and holding snakes. The significance of bull images, representing the god of fertility, in this mainly agricultural community are reminiscent of similar traditions noted in the Anatolian settlement of Alaca Hüyük. The snakes represent the chthonic god of the underworld and are associated with the annual cycle of regeneration: snakes were observed to disappear into the ground in winter (hibernation) and re-emerge (rebirth) the following spring.

Another model, depicting two pairs of oxen drawing ploughs, shows that some agricultural techniques have remained essentially unchanged for some 4000 years.

Other grave finds, including articles of gold, glass beads, and cylinder seals, suggest trading links with Syria and Egypt. Flat, card shaped idols with incised designs are also characteristic of the Early Bronze Age.

Middle Bronze Age (1900 - 1600 BC)

This period is marked by an upsurge in cultural and trading contacts with neighbouring countries. Copper was now a major export commodity, supporting the development of large towns such as Enkomi. Indeed some scholars believe that Enkomi is the copper rich Alasia referred to in Assyrian and Babylonian texts. The extent of trade is revealed by tomb finds of Egyptian faience beads, Asian cylinder seals, and Minoan vases, whilst Cypriot pottery has turned up in Cilicia and Palestine, and as far afield as Crete.

Parallel to this increasing prosperity was a growing insecurity on the island, caused perhaps by internal conflict, or influenced by events on the mainland, where the Hyksos had overrun Egypt, Palestine and northern Syria. Fortresses began to appear such as that at Krini, and Nitovikla in the Karpas peninsular.

In the potters workshop the *red polished ware* was supplanted by the *white painted* style, with variations according to locality. In the Karpas, *red on black ware* was developed.

Late Bronze Age (1650 - 1050 BC)

The destruction of the Hyksos Kingdom and the revival of Egypt as the leading power in the eastern Mediterranean created for Cyprus, at the beginning of the Late Bronze Age, favourable circumstances for its development into a flourishing commercial centre. The island also became a stepping stone for eastern and western cultural exchange.

The advent of Mycenaean traders, who took over from the Minoan Cretans, introduced a Greek element which left a permanent imprint on the cultural development of the island, and which entered into a fruitful dialogue with the neighbouring oriental cultures. These Mycenaeans, who settled in the Late Bronze Age towns of Enkomi, Hala Sultan Tekke, Paphos and Kition, brought with them a style of pottery whose figurative designs of warriors and chariots, fishes and birds, were highly prized in the Levant.This style constitutes the main mass of Late Bronze Age pottery, but its production, aimed at oriental markets and tastes, was largely confined to Mycenaean centres.

The period between 1500 and 1200 BC saw the fusion of design elements from both East and West into the traditional Cypriot forms as evinced in finds at Enkomi, Akdeniz (Ayia Irini), and Toumba tou Skourou. Religious practices too combine elements from both the Orient and the Aegean.

Around 1500 BC, a script similar to the *Linear A* found in Crete, appeared, known now as *Cypro-Minoan* script.

The prosperity of the Late Bronze Age, as reflected in tomb and city architecture as well as rich grave finds, was disrupted at the end of the 13th century by the so-called *sea people*, whose origin is still a matter of conjecture. Cities were abandoned or fortified, destroyed and rebuilt. The turbulence of the period is revealed by the increased number of swords and other weapons found in the graves.

BIRD FACED GODDESS

At the same time, following the Dorian invasion of Mycenaean centres in the Pelloponese, Achaean settlers landed on the coasts of Cyprus. This Achaean colonisation is the historical basis connecting the Trojan war with the foundation of certain Cypriot cities by Trojan heroes. Thus Salamis was believed to have been founded by Teucer, Paphos by Agpenor of Tegea, Soli by Akamas, and Lapta by Praxanor of Laconia.

The newcomers brought with them their burial customs, and Mycenaean chamber tombs can be seen alongside the traditional Cypriot graves. Terracotta figures of a female deity with upraised arms, reminiscent of Cretan models have been found in these tombs. In Enkomi the figure of a god wearing a horned helmet and standing on an ingot of copper was recovered, and has been identified by some as *Apollo Kereates*, an idol of the shepherds of Arcadia.

Geometric Period (1050 - 750 BC)

The transition to the Iron Age was for Cyprus, as for Greece, a dark age. Natural catastrophes destroyed nearly all the Late Bronze Age settlements and

'HORNED GOD' STATUETTE

led to a cultural decline, poverty, and a slump in population. Nevertheless archaeologists have found traces of a continuity of culture and the traditions of both the Eteocypriots and the Cypro-Mycenaeans.

It was not until the arrival of the Phoenicians that the island received a fresh cultural impulse, resulting in strengthened links with the Orient. The Phoenician colonisers arrived in Cyprus from Tyre in the 9th century BC, and came to dominate the city states of Idalion, Amathus, Kition and Lapithos.

The Phoenicians brought with them the cult of Astarte, the goddess of love and fertility, and in 800 BC, they replaced the Mycenaean temple at Kition with a sanctuary to Astarte. The Greek cult of Aphrodite incorporates features of the Astarte cult which suggests that the transformation of Astarte into Aphrodite occurred in Cyprus.

In ceramics, the pottery of the Bronze Age was augmented by two styles of Phoenician ware: *Black on Red* and *Red Slip*. The Phoenician influence is also apparent in metalwork, with silver bowls engraved and worked in relief designs, and bronze pieces with gold inlay.

Archaic Period (750 - 475 BC)

In the 8th century BC, Cyprus was once more drawn into the realm of the Near-Eastern powers.

Under Sargon II (721 - 705 BC), Cypriot cities paid tribute to the Assyrian Kingdom, and after an Egytian interlude (560 - 525 BC), were incorporated into the fifth satrapy of the Persian Empire. Their Persian masters allowed the Cypriot cities considerable latitude, and created, as the *pax Egyptica* had done a thousand years earlier, favourable conditions for an economic and cultural resurgence. Owing to its geographical position, and its natural wealth in copper and wood, the island flourished.

Several city states had the right to mint their own coins, including, in the north, Lapithos, Salamis, Soli, and Chytri. Cypriots adopted the art and luxurious lifestyle of the East, and the extravant fusion of cultures is demonstrated by the Royal Tombs, which reflect the high point of this cultural synthesis.

Gods of the Greeks, the Egyptians and the Phoenicians, amongst them Apollo, Heracles, Zeus, Ptah, Hathor, Baal, Melkarth, and Reshef all found found followers on the island.

In a temenos near Akdeniz (Ayia Irini), more than 2000 terra-cotta figures were found - some of them life-size - grouped about an altar. Some are evidently icons of deities, but some have singular

BICHROME WARE
'FREE FIELD' STYLE

12

features which suggest that real persons were represented.

In pottery, the bichrome style continued, but decorated now with plant and floral motifs. Pots freely painted with imaginative creatures, animals and people, known as the *Free Field Style*, and derived from Phoenician influence, demonstrate the exuberance of the times.

Classical Period (475 - 325 BC)

The flowering of the Archaic epoch was interrupted by external events into which the island was drawn on account of its geographical situation. The uprising of the coastal towns of Asia Minor against the Persians in 499 BC led to a polarisation in Cyprus of the pro Greek and pro Persian cities. Matters came to a head when the pro Persian king of Salamis, Gorgos, was deposed by his younger brother Onesilos, who gathered islandwide support, (with the exception of Amathus, a Phoenician city), to throw off the Persian yoke. The revolt was crushed and Onesilos perished, though his allies, the Ionians, were more successful at sea, demolishing the Phoenician fleet.

The Delian League, set up by Greeks to regain territory lost to the Persians, saw Cyprus important both strategically, and as a source of materials, especially timber. In 478 BC, Pausanias the Spartan succeeded in temporarily liberating large parts of the island, but this and subsequent attempts ultimately failed.

At the end of the 5th century BC, Evagoras, a descendant of Teucer, seized the throne of Salamis from the Persian puppet Abdemon. Whilst maintaining good relations with the Persians, Evagoras promoted Greek culture, and developed Salamis into thriving and powerful city. However, when he tried to extend his authority throughout Cyprus, the Persians intervened, and after assistance from Athens and Egypt evaporated, he eventually capitulated. He retained possession of Salamis, paying tribute to the king of Persia. After his murder in 374 BC, his successors continued the struggle against the Persians until Alexander the Great destroyed the Persian Empire.

Whilst Evagoras propagated Greek art and civilization, former influences were by no means abandoned. Oriental traditions remained strong in the field of architecture, in the workshops of the gold and silver smiths, in ceramic design, and in other art forms.

13

Hellenistic Period (325 - 58 BC)

Alexanders armies swept through Asia Minor and defeated the Persian forces at Issus. When he marched south and laid siege to Tyre, the kings of Cyprus sent over 220 ships to help blockade the city. Alexander continued his campaign to Egypt, where he founded the city of Alexandria, before marching east to the Indus. However, he died at the age of 33, and the new independence enjoyed by Cyprus and its city kingdoms was short lived as it became embroiled in the struggles of succession.

The three Macedonian generals Antigonus, Seleucus, and Ptolemy divided the conquests of Alexander between them, but Cyprus was claimed by both Antigonus and Ptolemy. In 318 BC, Ptolemy established his control over most of the island, leaving his brother Menelaus in charge. However, in 306 BC, Demetrius, the son of Antigonus, landed at Carpasia and eventually mastered the island, holding it until 295 BC, when it was retaken by Ptolemy.

Under the first three Ptolemies, Alexandria became a centre of learning and of trade. Some of this rubbed off on Cyprus, though of course affecting only the upper echelons of society. The city kingdoms, which had enjoyed relative autonomy under the Assyrians and the Persians, now came under a central governor, or strategos, based in Paphos. However, cultural and religious institutions remained largely untouched by the Ptolemies, though the local syllabary was gradually supplanted by the Greek alphabet.

The importance of Cyprus as a shipping and trading centre at this time is symbolised by the wreck of a Greek cargo ship, recovered by archaeologists off the north coast, and now preserved with its contents in Kyrenia castle. The economic upswing found architectural expression in an ambitious building program which fundamentally changed the face of the cities. But little remains of the temples, forums, gymnasiums, and theatres that constituted the hub of each Hellenistic town: in Salamis, as in other Cypriot towns, Roman buildings were built on the ruins of their hellenic predecessors. However, many statues of limestone and terracotta did survive, depicting deities, state officials and leading citizens, carved in the Cypro-classical style.

One of the leading minds of the Hellenistic period was Zeno, the founder of Stoic philosophy. Born in Citium, this Cypriot went to Athens where he studied classical philosophy which he rejected as being impractical. He then developed a system of pragmatic materialism, which was more appropriate to the needs of the day.

The latter period of Ptolemaic rule degenerated into a series of internecine squabbles, and the insolent behaviour of the last Ptolemy towards a Roman senator, who was later elected tribune, gave Rome an excuse to annex the island. Marcus Portius Cato arrived in 58 BC to implement the annexation, and Cyprus became a province of the Roman Empire.

Roman Period (58 BC - AD 330)

The decline of the Hellenistic states coincided with the rise of Rome as a regional power.

The period of some 30 years up to 30 BC was marked by the struggle for power in Rome. The senate had lost its authority to the generals, who strove amongst themselves for supreme power. Julius Caesar eventually crushed his rival Pompey and assumed the dictatorship, determined to reform the government of the empire. His assassination in 44 BC was followed by disorder until Octavian, Caesar's great nephew, vanquished his opponents and ascended to power as Emperor Augustus.

Cyprus was initially included in the province of Cilicia, but after briefly reverting to Egyptian control, it was in 22 BC classified as a senatorial province, and administered by a proconsul and his staff, who resided in Paphos.

Augustus implemented many of the reforms initiated by Caesar, including abolishing the farming out of tax collection, which had led to the impoverishment of subject and treasury alike. This reform allowed the government to spend extensively on public works without oppressing the peasant purse.

In Cyprus a large scale building program was expedited. New harbours were built, roads were laid, aqueducts were constructed to channel water to the cities which were equipped with temples, market places, theatres, and other public amenities. The massive stone forum at Salamis is the largest Roman market place known, and indeed that city became prodigiously wealthy, exporting copper and oil, wheat and wine to the markets of Rome.

In AD 46 Paul and Barnabas, a native of Salamis, travelled to Paphos where they revealed the gospel to the Roman governor Sergius Paulus. He was converted and thus became the worlds first Christian ruler. Barnabas later preached in Salamis where he was eventually martyred by the Jews.

The mission of Paul and Barnabas was to have far reaching implications, enabling the church in later years to demonstrate its apostolic origin and justifying its claim to be autocephalous and independent of the patriarch of Antioch.

After their revolt was crushed in Jerusalem in AD 70 by the Romans, many Jews settled in Cyprus, particularly in Salamis. Here, in AD 115, they rebelled again, and the ensuing carnage over the next two years prompted the decree from Rome expelling all Jews from the island.

For the next 50 years Cyprus enjoyed unparalleled prosperity, but the plague of AD 164, and the later degeneration of the Roman Empire left the country in a sorry plight. Fortunes revived under Constantine the Great (324-337), who tried to bind his empire together with the glue of Christianity, but in AD 364 the empire split, the eastern half being

ROMAN AMPHORA

ruled from the new capital city of Constantinople, located on the Bosporus.

Byzantine Period (330 - 1191)

With the foundation of Constantinople as the Roman capital in the East, the recipe was writ for a synthesis of Roman civic thought, Greek philosophy, and oriental Christian religion.

Earthquakes rocked the island of Cyprus in 332 and 342, tumbling the towns of Salamis, Kition and Paphos. Salamis, resuming its role as capital, was rebuilt by Constantius II (337-361), and renamed Constantia.

Since its adoption by Constantine as the official religion, Christianity spread rapidly throughout the empire. In 431 a dispute arose between the bishops of Cyprus and the patriarch of Antioch, who claimed ecclesiastical jurisdiction over the island. The autocephalous status of the Church of Cyprus was eventually confirmed by the Byzantine Emperor Zeno in 488, after Anthemios, bishop of Constantia, presented Zeno with reliquies of St.Barnabas, the location of which was revealed to him in a dream.

The standing of Cyprus and its significance to Byzantium is indicated by the decision of Emperor Justinian (527-565) to classify the island as a separate province. At this time, the cultivation of silk worms was developed, and this activity is recalled today by the widespread presence of mulberry trees.

BYZANTINE ARMS

For the next hundred years Cyprus lay quiet and undisturbed by the far off battles against Goth and Vandal, Persian and Slav. But out of the wastes of Arabia a new and potent power was gathering its forces. Islam spread like a forest fire throughout Syria, Palestine, and Egypt, and in 647 an Arab fleet of 1700 ships appeared off Salamis, led by Muawiya, the Emir of Syria and founder of the Omeyyad Caliphate. The city was sacked, and other towns were plundered and burned. From the 7th to the 9th century the island was repeatedly subject to Arab raids, and at times, tribute was paid to the Caliphate as well as taxes to Constantinople. During this period many towns were abandoned, and most ancient and early Christian buildings were destroyed. The inhabitants of Salamis/Constantia finally moved out and settled in Arsinoe, which later became Famagusta.

The devastation did not end until Emperor Nicephoros Phocas (963-969) finally gained the ascendency, driving the Moslem invaders from Cyprus and other parts of his realm. To protect the island from further incursion, the 11th century mountain castles of St.Hilarion, Buffavento, and Kantara were built. In addition, new fortifications for Kyrenia and Nicosia were constructed.

The 11th and 12th centuries were for Cyprus a period of renewed prosperity, which was expressed in the abundance of building works undertaken. The domed, cross shaped style of church became common, and also a multi-domed variety.

In the 11th century a new threat arose: Seljuk Turks swarmed in from the east, seizing the crumbling Caliphate, capturing Jerusalem (1071), and crushing the Byzantine emperor at the battle of Manzikert. Taking advantage of the weakened condition of the empire, Isaac Comnenos, a nephew of Emperor Manuel Comnenus, usurped control of Cyprus with the aid of false documents in 1184. He crowned himself emperor, renouncing his allegiance to Constantinople.

The Lusignan Dynasty (1192 - 1489)

The Lusignans came to rule Cyprus as a result of the Crusades. Alexius Comnenus became emperor of Byzantium in 1081, and despite the Great Schism of 1054 which split the church in two, he sought help from Pope Urban II to drive the Turks from Asia Minor. This led to the Crusades, which the Roman church saw as a means of extending its power, and others saw as a means to booty.

By the end of the century Christian forces occupied territory stretching from Edessa to Egypt, and had established the Kingdom of Jerusalem.

In 1186 the French adventurer Guy de Lusignan ascended the throne of Jerusalem by virtue of marriage to Sybilla, the heiress of the kingdom. By this time the great Saladin had welded the Moslem nations together and embarked on a *jihad* to recover Jerusalem. He destroyed Guy's armies in 1187 and then took Jerusalem, leaving only Tyre, and the principalities of Tripoli and Antioch in Christian hands.

The news of the fall of Jerusalem shocked the European powers, who organized the Third Crusade. The Germans went by land, but the French, led by Philip II, and the English, led by Richard the Lionheart elected to travel by sea to Acre. On the way, Richard's fleet was scattered by a storm: several ships foundered off the coast of Cyprus, and the one in which Richard's fiancée was sailing, took refuge in the harbour at

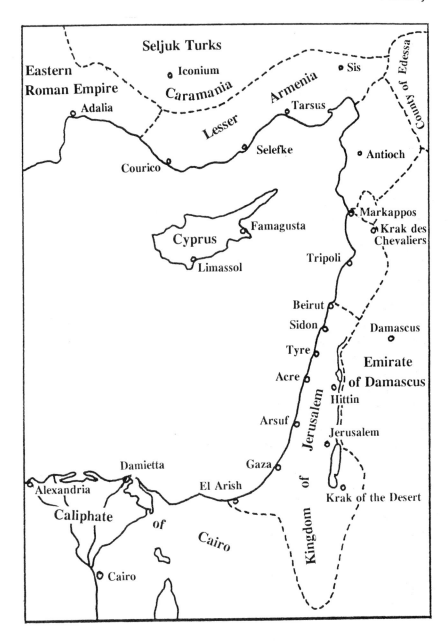

MAP OF EASTERN MEDITERRANEAN PRIOR TO SALADIN'S CONQUESTS

Limassol. The year was 1191, and the self proclaimed emperor Isaac Comnenos was ruling Cyprus. He made the fatal mistake of arresting Richard's shipwrecked sailors, and abusing his fiancée Berengaria. When Richard arrived a few days later, he landed in force, and seized Limassol. Isaac capitulated, and swore allegiance to Richard, but immediately broke his oath, and fled to Kantara. He was eventually captured at Cape Andreas in the Karpas by Guy de Lusignan, who had arrived in Cyprus to join Richard.

On May 12th 1191, Richard married Berengaria of Navarre in Limassol, and she was crowned Queen of England.

In June, with bulging treasure chests filled with the wealth Isaac had amassed during his rule, Richard set sail for Acre, leaving a garrisoned Cyprus in the charge of Richard of Camville and Robert of Tornham. These two were soon occupied in suppressing a revolt of their unwilling subjects and on hearing the news, King Richard sold the island to a military order of knights, the Templars, for 100,000 bezants.

The Templars soon discovered that the rebellious Cypriots would not submit to their severe rule, and after desperately putting down a popular uprising, they begged Richard to cancel their purchase.

On the death of his wife Sybilla, Guy de Lusignan's claim to the crown of Jerusalem weakened, and he was deposed by the barons. To compensate his loss, Richard offered him the island of Cyprus, and thus began the Lusignan dynasty, which was to endure for 300 years.

Guy introduced the feudal system, granting estates to the barons who had accompanied him from Palestine. Constitutional and legal matters were dealt with by the Assizes of Jerusalem, a code adopted from the former kingdom, but local laws and customs were retained.

Two years later, in 1194, Guy died and he was succeeded by his brother Amaury. To ratify his right to rule, Amaury obtained a crown from the Holy Roman Emperor, Henry VI, and in 1197 became the first Lusignan king of Cyprus. To secure his position from without and within, Amaury extended the mountain castles of St.Hilarion, Buffavento, and Kantara. He also took steps to displace the Orthodox church, introducing the Roman communion.

Oppression of the Orthodox church was supplemented in 1222 by decrees issued at the Council of Famagusta: the Orthodox sees were reduced, and the four remaining bishops packed off to country towns; Orthodox revenues were allocated to the Latin church, and in general, the Orthodox church was placed in a Latin strait-jacket.

The suppression of their religion was not the only hardship suffered by the local population. Contemporary travellers noted the stark contrast between the extravagant luxury enjoyed by the upper echelons, and the grinding poverty endured by the peasants. Frederick II, the Holy Roman Emperor and son of Henry VI, landed in Cyprus in 1228 on his way to Palestine, to assert his rights as suzerain. He immediately fell into conflict with Jean d'Ibelin, Lord of Beirut and regent of Cyprus during the minority of young King Henry. A compromise was reached whereby Jean d'Ibelin accompanied Frederick on his crusade, and Sir Amalric Barlais, a favourite of Queen Alix (Henry's mother), was appointed regent, along with four other barons.

With Jean d'Ibelin absent, Sir Amalric took steps to consolidate his position, confiscating the properties of his rival. Returning to Cyprus, Jean d'Ibelin defeated his enemy in battle outside Nicosia. Sir Amalric retreated to St. Hilarion, but eventually surrendered after a long siege, and relinquished his claim to the regency.

ARMS OF THE KINGS OF CYPRUS & JERUSALEM

Emperor Frederick II was by now back in Europe, after achieving notable success on his crusade by skilful negotiations with the Arabs. He now sent his marshall, Richard Filangeri, to destroy the d'Ibelins in Cyprus and Palestine. In 1232 Filangeri took Beirut and invested the citadel. Jean d'Ibelin sailed over in force from Cyprus to relieve his city, but wily Filangeri sent imperial forces under the renegade Amalric Barlais to Cyprus, where he overran the island. Jean d'Ibelin returned to Cyprus, defeating the enemy and blockading them in Kyrenia castle for over a year, before Frederick withdrew his troops.

The fall of Jerusalem in 1244 provoked the disastrous 7th Crusade, led by King Louis of France. Accompanying his party were a number of architects, artists and stone masons. Some of these remained in Cyprus and were instrumental in the creation of the Gothic masterworks in this period.

21

After the death of King Henry in 1253, and his young heir in 1267, Hugh of Antioch ascended the throne as Hugh III. His exceptional qualities inspired Thomas Aquinas to write his *"De Regimine Principum"*. (For the Guidance of Princes). He took effective action during the plague and famine of 1267, and under his rule the country prospered. He was a generous patron of Bellapais Abbey, but when he died in 1284, he was buried in St. Sophia cathedral in Nicosia.

The principal event during the reign of Henry II (1285-1324) was the fall of Acre in 1291. The last crusader stronghold in the Levant was lost, and Cyprus became the Christian outpost of the East. Genoese, Venetian and other merchants transferred their establishments to Famagusta, which rapidly flourished as the major trade centre linking occident and orient. In the 14th century Famagusta became one of the wealthiest and most influential cities in the Mediterranean.

This prosperity was disturbed during the reign of Hugh IV (1324-1358) by the havoc wrought by the bubonic plague or 'Black Death' of 1349. The king sought refuge in St.Hilarion, trade ground to a halt, and after the pestilence, the population was so depleted that many a merchant was raised to fill the ranks of the nobility.

The Lusignan dynasty reached the zenith of its glory under Peter I, who was crowned king of Cyprus and Jerusalem in 1358. In Asia Minor at this time, the Armenian kingdom had been all but overrun by the Ottoman Turks. In response to pleas for help, Peter sent relief to the Armenians in Courico, and then successfully stormed the mighty Turkish fortress at Adalia.

However, his main purpose in life was to re-establish the kingdom of Jerusalem, and to this end he toured Europe in 1362, hoping to drum up support for his venture. Enthusiasm for the crusades had waned in Europe, and only a small contingent accompanied him when he eventually set sail from Venice in 1365. Peter landed at Rhodes, to join forces with the Hospitallers, who had made that island their headquarters, and then sailed to Egypt, the seat of Moslem power.

Alexandria was taken by surprise and pillaged, but his forces would venture no further in the face of a powerful Mameluke army, so Peter retired to Cyprus, hoping to gather more knights from Europe to prosecute the cause. The apathetic response of European nobility, and the eagerness of merchants to resume trade with the East, caused Pope Urban V to advise Peter to make peace with Egypt.

King Peter turned his attention to Asia Minor, where the Caramanian Turks were advancing upon Courico. As negotiations with Egypt were still under way, Peter sent his brother, the Prince of Antioch to relieve the town. His success was total: learning that the Turks intended to retire pending the outcome of events in Egypt, the prince pounced and the Turks were routed. Meanwhile, to induce the Egyptians to speed up negotiations, King Peter pillaged towns along the Syrian coast, and soon a peace treaty was signed. In 1369 Peter was assassinated, and was succeeded by his young son Peter II.

Rivalries between the mercantile powers erupted at the coronation of Peter II as king of Jerusalem and Cyprus in Famagusta in 1372. A dispute between the representatives of Genoa and Venice as to who should lead the king's horse resulted in a brawl, and the hostilities were continued after the celebrations when the Venetians, with tacit Cypriot support, attacked the Genoese, killing several, and destroying their property.

The Genoese responded with an iron fist. Troops were despatched, Famagusta and Nicosia were seized, along with the young king. James, the constable of Cyprus, and Eleanor, the king's mother, retired to Kyrenia castle which withstood all Genoese assaults. A treaty in 1374 restored Peter to the throne, but Famagusta was retained by the Genoese, and James was kept hostage in Genoa until he succeeded to the throne in 1385.

In 1396, James I added the title of king of Armenia to those of king of Jerusalem and Cyprus, but the honour increased neither his wealth nor his territory.

The raids on Egypt by Janus (1398-1432), aroused the wrath of the Mamelukes, who descended upon Cyprus in 1426 and annihilated a plague weakened Cypriot army, sacked Nicosia, and imposed tribute on the island.

The Lusignan dynasty never recovered. Intrigue within the royal family further weakened its position. The illegitimate usurper James II (1460-1473) managed to wrest Famagusta from the declining Genoese, but his marriage to Caterina Cornaro of Venice was a fatal error. The Venetians, who had long coveted the island, soon engineered the king's death, and effectively ruled Cyprus until they officially took over in 1489, when Queen Caterina was persuaded to relinquish her position in their favour.

In terms of art, the era of the Lusignans and the crusaders was one of the most brilliant and significant epochs in the history of Cyprus. The Gothic churches and cathedrals, the Abbey at Bellapais, the crusader castles of St.Hilarion, Buffavento and Kantara, all constitute the most impressive memorial to Frankish art of the middle ages on oriental soil.

Decisive to the development of Franco-Cypriot Gothic architecture was the visit in 1248 of Louis IX of France, who brought with him master builders and stonemasons versed in the styles current in the Champagne, and the Ile de France. The fall of Acre and the consequent cosmopolitan influx introduced Italian and Catalan elements into Cypriot gothic art. After the marriage of King John II (1432-1458) to the Byzantine princess Helena Palaeologa, which reinforced the Byzantine aspect of the island, the Byzantine and Gothic style elements combined to create a composite architecture whose influence has extended up to the 20th century.

Venetian Period (1489 - 1571)

The Venetian desire for Cyprus was inspired purely by profit. The island was well endowed with the timber essential for shipbuilding, and formed an ideal base from which the Venetians could dominate trade with the east. They continued to pay the tribute enforced upon Cyprus by the Mamelukes, and when the latter were conquered by the Ottomans, the tribute was redirected to Constantinople, the seat of Ottoman power since 1453.

Anticipating conflict, the Venetians undertook an ambitious plan of fortification. Famagusta and Nicosia were ringed with massive earthworks, cased with stone. An outer wall was erected around Kyrenia castle, the gap being filled with earth to form an artillery rampart. The best military architects in Europe were brought in to design and execute these projects.

LION OF ST. MARK

All was in vain. A body blow had already been dealt to Venice by Bartholemew Diaz, who in 1486 discovered a new sea route to India via the Cape of Good Hope. In 1570, after an ultimatum from Sultan Selim II had expired, hordes of Ottoman troops landed at Larnaca, under Lala Mustapha Pasha. Nicosia was invested, and resisted for six weeks, refusing terms of honourable surrender on rumours of an approaching Venetian fleet. The city was eventually taken by storm, and sacked, 20,000 inhabitants being massacred in the process. Kyrenia capitulated without a struggle. In October of 1570, Lala Mustapha Pasha with an army of 200,000, began the siege of Famagusta. The beleaguered party received meagre reinforcements in January 1571, when the Turkish fleet withdrew to winter anchorage, but after ten months the garrison was reduced to 1500 men, whilst 80,000 Ottoman soldiers had perished. On August 1st, terms of capitulation were agreed between the captain of Famagusta, Marc Antonio Bragadino, and Lala Mustapha Pasha. However, a dispute arose and some incautious words by Bragadino resulted in his being flayed alive.

Later that month Venetian officials handed over the island together with 300,000 ducats for war reparation.

October of 1571 saw a European League fleet destroy the Turkish fleet at Lepanto, but by this time Cyprus was lost and was to remain a backwater of the Ottoman Empire for the next 300 years.

Turkish Rule (1571 - 1878)

The takeover by the Ottoman Empire in 1571 was largely welcomed by the local population, who had to some extent collaborated with the invaders, and who anticipated changes for the better. To begin with, their hopes were justified. The hated Latin church was uprooted, with many churches being converted into mosques, and the Orthodox church was restored to dominance. The feudal system was abolished, and the former serfs could now own and inherit land.

The population at this time, according to an official census, was 150,000. In addition to these rayahs, or non Moslems, there were also some 30,000 Turkish settlers, who were granted land by the Sultan, and changed the demographic nature of the island.

Although the Sultan and high officials at the Porte in Constantinople may sincerely have wished fair treatment for their subjects, the system of government was open to abuse. Cyprus was ruled by a three plumed Pasha, who was installed as governor in Nicosia, with two plumed Pashas placed in Paphos and Famagusta. Turkish settlers and rayahs alike were subject to taxes which were gathered by the aghas. These aghas purchased their positions from the Porte, and were naturally energetic in their efforts to extract taxes from the people, in order to offset their expenditure, and realize a fat profit. The Cypriots thus succeeded merely in exchanging one form of oppression for another. Natural catastrophes added to their woes, and by 1641, with plague following close on the heels of famine, the total population had plummeted to 25,000. The Porte sought to alleviate the situation by reducing taxation, and more importantly recognizing, albeit unofficially, the Orthodox archbishop as the representative of the rayahs.

Conditions did not improve when, in 1702, Cyprus became the fief of the Grand Vizier. The post of governor was sold on an annual basis, and the incumbent made it his business to end his tenure on a wealthy note.

17TH C. OTTOMAN ARMS

Temporary relief came in 1746 when Abu Bekr Pasha ruled the country. This enlightened man undertook many public works, and at his own expense built the aqueduct which supplied Larnaca with water for the next 200 years.

In 1754 the Sultan recognised the Orthodox archbishop as Ethnarch, or leader of the Cypriot community, and granting him and his bishops various privileges, along with the responsibility of collecting taxes. As the century progressed, the bishops' power and wealth increased as they cynically worked hand in glove with the Turkish governors. Both Greek and Turkish peasants revolted in vain against the rapacity of their masters.

In 1821 the archbishop, along with other clergy and leading Christians, were discovered to have connections with the secret organization Filika Eteria, a Greek nationalist movement aimed at driving the Turks from Greece. The response of the governor Küçük Mehmet was swift and bloody. The archbishop, the bishops, and many prominent Christians were massacred, and this was followed by an islandwide purge of the Christians. Some escaped by fleeing the country, or by taking refuge with the European consuls in Larnaca.

Meanwhile the vast Ottoman Empire was showing signs of disintegration. After crushing the Greek revolt with the help of the Egyptian governor, Mohammed Ali, the European powers intervened, resulting in the creation of an independent Greek Kingdom in 1832. At the same, time Mohammed Ali inflicted defeat on his Ottoman masters and established an independent dynasty in Egypt.

In the midst of these troubles, Sultan Mahmoud II instituted reforms which alleviated the condition of his subjects, including those in Cyprus. The farming of taxes was abolished, but external problems impeded the implementation of this and other reforms.

War with Russia, which had continued off and on since 1769, when the Russians won access through the Bosporus, was weakening the Ottoman Empire, and after further defeats in 1877, chunks of Anatolia were ceded to the Russians. This alarmed the English, who saw the Russian advance as a threat to the Suez canal which had been opened in 1869. An agreement was subsequently reached in 1878 whereby England would occupy Cyprus, using it as a base to protect her own interests, and to defend Ottoman territory against further encroachments by Russia.

COURTYARD OF A PRIVATE HOUSE (SALVATOR)

27

British Rule (1878 - 1960)

Had Britain taken military control of Egypt five years earlier than it did (in 1882), it is quite likely that there would have been no strategic grounds for occupying Cyprus. However, history cast a lifeline to that island adrift, and drew it alongside the flagship of modern Europe.

Under the convention of occupation, Cyprus was still a part of the Ottoman empire, and the excess of revenue over expenditure, agreed at £92,000, was paid annually to the Sultan.

The first High Commissioner, Sir Garnet Wolseley, took steps to create a new constitution. A Legislative Council was formed, and a High Court was established in Nicosia, presided over by two British judges. The district courts were served by one Christian and one Moslem judge, under the supervision of a British official. In 1882 the Legislative Council, formerly consisting of four British, and three local members, was modified to comprise six British officials, and twelve elected local members. The proportion of the latter, three Turkish and nine Greek Cypriots, caused an inverse proportion of outrage. However, in practice, the Turks generally sided with the British officials, and in the event of a tie, the High Commissioner cast the deciding vote. The tax system was drastically restructured, and the change of emphasis from direct to indirect taxes served to increase revenues whilst leaving more money in the peasant pocket.

The British undertook an extensive program of public works, including the construction of roads and bridges, drinking and irrigation water supplies, and even a railway line linking Nicosia to Famagusta and Güzelyurt (Morphou). In addition, port facilities were improved, and administration buildings, schools and hospitals were built.

When Turkey sided with Germany in World War I, Britain annexed the island, annulling the convention of 1878. In 1915, Great Britain offered Cyprus to Greece in return for joining the allied cause, but the suggestion was rejected, and with it the chance of *enosis*, the striving for which would cause so much strife in the future. Ten years later, Cyprus became a Crown Colony, and the High Commissioner was replaced by a Governor.

Meanwhile, the *enosis* movement, aiming for union with Greece, was growing within the Greek Cypriot community, fostered by the powerful Orthodox church. The movement erupted into islandwide riots in 1931, during which Government House was burnt to the ground. The uprising was crushed, and the Legislative Council abolished thus eliminating the local voice in government decisions.

After World War II, when 30,000 Cypriots fought in the British army, calls for *enosis* were renewed. A plebicite organized in 1950 by Makarios, later Archbishop Makarios III, showed that 96% ofthe Greek Cypriots supported union with Greece. However, it has been reported that excommunication was a stick used to encourage the overwhelming vote. Furthermore, it is doubtful that many Cypriots understood the full

implications of *encsis*, quite apart from the fact that it was anathema to the Turkish Cypriot minority.

Post war attitudes were against the old ideas of colonialism, and when Greek Cypriot demands for self determination resulted only in the offer of a new constitution, the signal was given for Colonel George Grivas, who used the name 'Dighenis', after the legendary Byzantine hero, to launch EOKA. (National Organization of Cypriot Fighters) This armed struggle against British rule began in April 1955, and was abetted in the churches by the clergy, with the blessing, indeed the leadership, of Archbishop Makarios III. The latter was deported to the Seychelles 14 months later after the call for *enosis* had been outlawed. The Turkish Cypriot community spawned their own movements: *taksim* called for the division of the island; TMT was the Turkish Cypriot resistance movement.

After a conference attended by Greece, Turkey and Britain in June 1955 failed to achieve a solution, Greece applied to the United Nations in 1957 and again in 1958, claiming the right of self determination for Cypriots. This claim, of course, did not take into account the position of the Turkish Cypriot minority, and as a counterthrust, Turkey suggested a *double enosis*, or partition of the island.

Meanwhile, Grivas and his terrorists were actively prosecuting their cause, undaunted by the emergency regulations, and with the total death toll rising above 500, the British were anxious to find a suitable formula for independence. This was eventually hammered out in the Treaty of Zurich, and on 19th February 1959, Makarios III, Dr. Fazıl Küçük (the Turkish Cypriot representative), plus the prime ministers of Britain, Greece, and Turkey, all signed the London Accord, granting Cyprus independence. The agreement, which left Britain with the sovereign base areas of Akrotiri and Dhekelia, provided guarantor powers of intervention to Britain, Greece, and Turkey.

The Republic of Cyprus came into being on 19th August 1960, and on 20th September it joined the United Nations, and the British Commonwealth.

Independent Cyprus and the Turkish Intervention

The constitution arising from the London Accord provided for a bi-communal society, with safeguards to prevent the majority Greek Cypriots from dominating the Turkish Cypriots.

Greece, Turkey, and Great Britain were assigned the guarantor powers, with the right to intervene militarily if the London Accord was breached. The president was to be from the Greek, and the vice-president from the Turkish community, each with the power of veto. In the government and the civil service, the communities were represented in the ratio of 70% to 30%, whilst in the police and army, the ratio was 60% to 40%. Failure to agree on the structure of the army resulted in Makarios, the first president of Cyprus, declaring that Cyprus would have no armed forces. This led to the formation of private armies, supplied clandestinely by Greece and Turkey.

In legislative matters, separate majorities were required from the Greek and Turkish members of the Cyprus House of Representatives. The major towns had separate municipalities, and in the law courts, the accused were tried by members of their own community.

This complicated system proved to be unworkable in practice, owing to inherent suspicions between the two communities. However, a straightforward 'democracy', or majority rule, was not applicable to Cyprus as it would have resulted in the Turkish community having no effective say in the government, and would have almost certainly have led to a declaration of *enosis*, or union with Greece.

In November 1963, Makarios submitted a plan to Dr. Küçük, the vice-president, aimed at simplifying the constitution. The changes proposed removed most of the checks and balances which had been built into the constitution to protect the minority Turkish community, and were of course unacceptable to the Turks.

To some extent Makarios was under pressure from EOKA, which, having achieved its initial goal of independence for Cyprus, was now pursuing what they regarded as the next logical step - *enosis*. From Athens, General Grivas, the terrorist chief of EOKA, fulminated against Makarios and incited his fanatical supporters to seize the initiative.

Matters came to a head on Christmas eve, when armed Greeks attacked a suburb of Nicosia, Küçük Kaymaklı (Omorphita), killing or

31

capturing those Turkish Cypriots inhabitants who were unable to escape. Armed conflict spread, with the Turkish Cypriots withdrawing into enclaves to defend themselves.

A buffer zone was set up and manned by British troops in a largely unsuccessful attempt to stop the fighting. These were later replaced by United Nations troops in March 1964.

Makarios revealed his true colours when on January 1st 1964 he announced the abrogation of the treaties signed in London, intending to establish self determination for Cypriots, which, as the Greeks were in the majority, would almost certainly lead to a proclamation of *enosis*. Under pressure from Britain and Turkey, Makarios repealed his announcement.

In August 1964, well armed Greek forces attempted to crush the Turks at Erenköy (Kokkina) on the north coast, in order to interrupt the flow of munitions from the Turkish mainland: they would undoubtedly have succeeded had not the Turkish air force intervened. This act added a new dimension to the conflict. Fear of Turkish intervention sobered the Greeks somewhat, and they settled down to systematic economic blockade of the Turkish enclaves. This situation amounted to partition, especially as the Turks were no longer able to participate in the government or civil service.

Further armed conflict in 1967 provoked Turkey to threaten military intervention, but with the takeover by the colonels in Greece, and the economic boom in Cyprus, the concept of *enosis* grew less attractive.

In January 1974, Grivas, who had returned to Cyprus earlier to take charge of the armed forces and head the terrorist group EOKA-B, died of a heart attack near Limassol. During the presidential elections of that year, Makarios clearly renounced the cause of *enosis*, and was re-elected with 95% of the cast votes. He subsequently ordered the withdrawal of mainland Greek officers, whereupon the National Guard, which was under the command of Greek officers, stormed the presidential palace in Nicosia. Makarios escaped, but this attempted coup, sponsored by the military junta in Greece, persuaded Turkey to intervene, as a guarantor power. On 20th July 1974, Turkish forces landed and occupied 40% of the island in the north. 150,000 Greek Cypriots fled to the south, and 50,000 Turkish Cypriots escaped to the north. Substantial Turkish forces remained in the north, and the civilian population increased after considerable migration from the Turkish mainland.

Intercommunal negotiations since 1974 have been fruitless, and in November 1983, Northern Cyprus declared itself independent as the Turkish Republic of Northern Cyprus. Recognised only by Turkey, the TRNC is hampered economically and has not prospered as much as the south.

The Turkish Cypriot President Rauf Denktash and the Greek Cypriot President George Vassiliou have in recent years pursued discussions under the auspices of the former UN Secretary General Peres de Cuellar, with a view to a federal solution to the Cyprus problem, but ingrained mutual suspicion stalled any progress.

This year (1992), further talks have taken place in New York with the new UN Secretary General, Boutros Ghali, but subsequent face to face discussions have so far failed to yield a compromise acceptable to both sides, and a comprehensive settlement in the foreseeable future seems unlikely. Any imposed solution, occasionally mooted, would probably be short lived: successful historical precedents for this option are rare.

KYRENIA / GIRNE

Kyrenia, with its Venetian castle and picturesque harbour, plus the backdrop of the Kyrenia range, is one of the most attractive towns in Cyprus.

In olden days, Kyrenia was a centre for the export of carobs, which were used as horse fodder. In this century of motorised traffic, the tall carob warehouses lining the harbour have been converted into cafes, restaurants, and hotels, but the atmosphere of a small harbour town has been retained.

Kyrenia is a popular place of abode for expatriate Englishmen who do not wish to spend their retirement in their cold, wet, and expensive home country. The town is provided with an Anglican church and a cemetary.

It also provides the tourist with an excellent base for exploring the surrounding district, as many places of interest are located nearby, some within walking distance. Prominent among these are Bellapais Abbey and St.Hilarion castle, though hikers to the latter sometimes wish they had opted for a hire car!

Frequent taxi and minibus services provide transport to Nicosia and Famagusta. There is also a ferry connection to the Turkish mainland.

History

The history of settlement in the Kyrenia district goes back to Neolithic times. Archaeologists have discovered Neolithic remains at *Ayios Epiktitos Vrysi* and Bronze Age cemetaries at *Karmi* and *Vounous*. Obsidian and pottery finds indicate waves of immigration from Anatolia and from the Syrian/Palestinian coast in prehistoric times.

Myth relates that Kyrenia was founded by Achaean immigrants, who named the town after *Kerynia*, a mountain in the Peloponnese.

Other stories attribute its foundation to the Phoenicians, who had already established trading stations on the north coast of Cyprus a thousand years before Christ.

Tomb finds to the south east of the harbour indicate the existence of settlements in Archaic and Classical times.

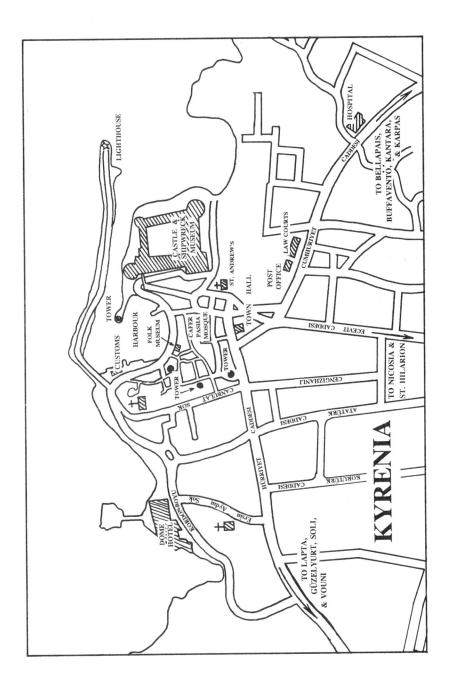

Cyprus had been annexed from the Ptolemies by the Romans in circa 50 BC. In 364 AD, the Roman Empire was divided between the east and the west, with Cyprus included in the Eastern Roman Empire, more commonly known as the Byzantine Empire.

Perpetual war with Persia weakened the Byzantine Empire, and from the 7th to the 10th centuries, it was unable protect Cyprus from the ravages of Arab pirates, and the invasions of the followers of Islam. Kyrenia was destroyed on several occasions, and it was not until the reign of Emperor Nicephoros Phocas (963-969) that the Moslems were finally driven from the island. At about this time, Kyrenia castle, and the mountain castles of St.Hilarion, Buffavento, and Kantara were built.

In 1191, during Richard the Lionheart's conquest of Cyprus, the daughter of the tyrant ruler Isaac Comnenos sought refuge in Kyrenia castle, but later submitted to the English king.

The traveller Willibrand von Oldenburg, who visited the island in 1211, wrote of a *"well fortified town with a castle with towers and strong walls,and a good harbour"*.

During the 12th and 13th centuries, the Byzantine castle was rebuilt by the Lusignans.

The Holy Roman Emperor, Frederick II, stopped in Cyprus in 1228 on his way to Palestine, to assert his authority on the island. He was the suzerain of the Lusignans, since Amaury, the first Lusignan king, had received his crown from Emperor Henry VI, Frederick's father.

Frederick immediately found himself in conflict with Jean d'Ibelin, lord of Beirut and uncle of Henry, the young king of Cyprus. Returning home after his crusade, Frederick sent out his marshall, Richard Filangeri, to crush the d'Ibelins in Syria and Cyprus.

Jean d'Ibelin, the most popular and respected Christian lord in the eastern Mediterranean, proved to be more than a match for Filangeri, and the imperial forces eventually retreated to Kyrenia castle in 1232. After a siege lasting more than a year, terms of peace were arranged: the castle was surrendered and prisoners were exchanged.

When in 1373 the Genoese overran the island and captured the boy King Peter II, the royalists fled to Kyrenia castle, which was put under siege in early 1374. Despite repeated attacks and the use of an immense stone throwing catapult, which demolished sections of the walls, the castle held out. The Genoese also tried to break through the harbour defences, but were repelled by the beleaguered party, under the command of James, the constable of Cyprus, who later ascended the throne.

King Janus, who succeeded his father James I, brought the wrath of the Mamelukes upon Cyprus, after his attacks on the shores of Egypt. After plundering Larnaca and Limassol in 1425, the Mamelukes returned a year later to annihilate the Cypriot army, capturing King Janus, and then sacked Nicosia. The king's brother Hugh and the rest of the royal family took refuge in Kyrenia castle.

The castle once again became a royal refuge in 1460 when Queen Charlotte, grand-daughter of King Janus, was blockaded there for nearly four years by her illegitimate brother. James usurped the throne, and his sister eventually fled to Rome with her husband.

After the Venetians took over the island in 1489, Kyrenia castle was converted into the artillery stronghold which survives today. During the Ottoman conquest of 1571, Kyrenia surrendered without a struggle on learning of the fall of Nicosia.

In 1765 Khalil, the Turkish commandant of Kyrenia castle, used the unrest caused by the imposition of certain taxes to try and seize the governorship of the island. He laid siege to Nicosia, but when the Porte in Constantinople sent Ahmed Pasha to quell the rebellion,he retired to Kyrenia castle. After 40 days, the blockaded castle was starved into submission. Khalil and his followers were executed, and Ahmed Pasha received his third plume in recognition of his successful campaign.

The British administration used the castle as a prison for captured EOKA terrorists.

Description of the castle

The Byzantine forerunner of the present castle was a much smaller structure consisting of four towers arranged in a square, joined by curtain walls encompassing a yard and ancilliary buildings erected against the walls. The castle was protected by a moat and provided with an inner harbour accessed from the main harbour through a large arch. A sea gate was available in the north wall, enabling the castle to be revictualled by ship when under seige. Additions and modifications were made during the Lusignan period, and when the Venetians took over the island, drastic alterations were made to prepare the castle for artillery warfare.

The original drawbridge has been replaced by a stone bridge of more recent vintage crossing the dry moat to the Venetian entrance. To the right of the entrance passage which leads to the Frankish gate, steps descend to the water gate. To the left, a passage leads back to a Byzantine church dating from the 12th century. The remnants of opus sectile flooring and marble columns with early Byzantine capitals suggest that an early Christian basilica once occupied this site. The church, given the name St.George of the Castle by the crusader knights who used it as the castle chapel, stood outside the walls of the Byzantine castle. It was integrated into the castle during the Venetian reconstruction.

Returning to the entrance passage, a ramp can be seen, up which artillery was hauled to the north west tower. This tower, added by the Venetians, protected the harbour and the north western part of the castle, and also afforded a good view over both the harbour and the town. Next to the artillery ramp is the old Frankish north west tower. Looking down from above, it can be seen from the stonework that the

38

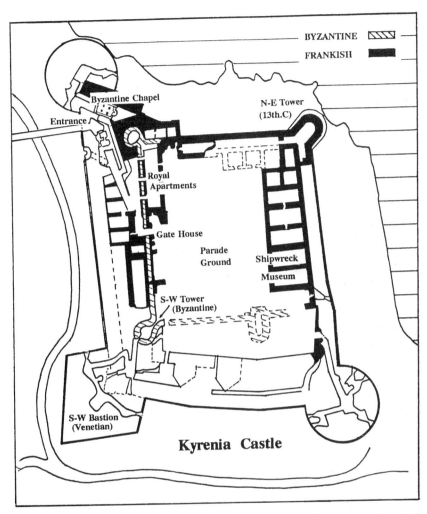

BYZANTINE ◻◻◻
FRANKISH ▬

Byzantine Chapel

Entrance

N-E Tower
(13th.C)

Royal
Apartments

Gate House

Parade
Ground

Shipwreck

Museum

S-W Tower
(Byzantine)

S-W Bastion
(Venetian)

Kyrenia Castle

original Byzantine tower was round: the square shape is a Frankish modification.

The 14th century Frankish gatehouse is also a replacement of an earlier Byzantine model. Above the gate, which was fitted with a portcullis, can be seen Lusignan coats of arms, these emblems being placed there in more recent times. The sarcophagus of the Ottoman admiral Sadik Pasha, who fell during the conquest of Cyprus stands before the Frankish guard rooms.

In the western side of the courtyard, sections of the old rough Byzantine walls survive. These were reinforced by the Franks and openings cut out to allow access to rooms which were built on behind, and which now accommodate the castle officials. Steps lead to the top floor where there was a latin chapel. The buildings to the north of the entrance were stables, and above them was a great hall, possibly royal apartments, with a window in the north wall above the portcullis gate; further windows looked out over the town and harbour. This hall was flanked on two sides with broad balconies overlooking the parade ground, judging from the substantial stone brackets projecting from the walls. Steps from the ground floor lead to storage chambers, powder rooms, and the dungeons. A torch is necessary for these explorations.

The remains of a round Byzantine tower can be seen near the south west corner of the courtyard. The tower is now totally enclosed, but a gangway leads through it down into the massive rhomboid Venetian south west bastion, which has cannon emplacements on several levels. This bastion would appear to be a later addition to the Venetian modifications, as the masonry work is different: the decorative external half-round beading is absent, and the walls do not appear to be keyed in with the principal corner.

The gap between the Byzantine and the Frankish south walls was filled in by the Venetians to form a gangway some 25 yards wide where the defenders could array themselves. In the south west corner is a little yard reached through a small passage; the portal on the inside, carved with three lions, dates from Roman times.

Facing the sea, the north wall with its lofty battlements is a product of Lusignan masons, though it follows the course of an earlier Byzantine wall. The castellations are noteworthy, the merlons being provided with arrow slits and embrasures for the archers. The Venetians made no alterations, considering the cliffs and the sea to be adequate allies. Rooms built against these walls served as barracks. The Frankish north east tower also survives unchanged, and consists of two tall rooms equipped with shooting slits set in vaulted recesses. Steps lead from here into the series of apartments comprising the east wing, also erected by the Lusignans, and now undergoing restoration. The southern section of this wing building now accommodates Shipwreck Museum.

Kyrenia castle, with its massive walls and mighty bastions, is one of the most impressive and best preserved fortresses in the Levant.

Shipwreck Museum

In 1965 a local diver noticed a shipwreck lying in 100 ft of water about a mile off the coast to the north east of Kyrenia. His discovery resulted in a major expedition of recovery by the University of Pennsylvania. The wreck was carefully excavated and photographed in great detail before being raised to the surface. The wooden ship was impregnated with a preservative resin before being displayed in a specially prepared hall in the east wing of the castle. A replica of the ship is also on display in the museum.

Estimated to be 2300 years old, the wreck is the most ancient to have been recovered from the sea bed. The 45 ft hull, made from Aleppo pine,was sheathed.in lead, a hitherto unknown technique which was probably employed to protect the timbers against Mediterranean sea worm.

The ships cargo included more than 400 amphorae from the islands of Rhodes and Samos, and 29 basalt mills from Cos. This suggests that the

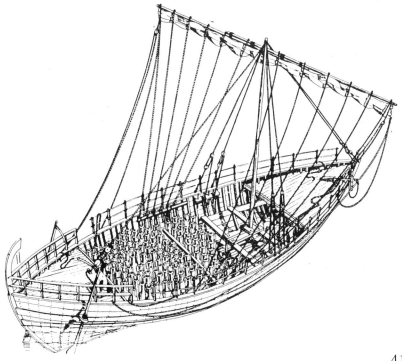

ship sailed along the coast of Asia Minor collecting goods before crossing to Cyprus. Utensils for four people were also found,implying a four man crew. According to carbon 14 analysis, almonds found on board were dated at 288 BC, plus or minus 62 years. The ship's timbers yielded a date of 389 BC plus or minus 44 years. This shows that the ship had been in use for at least 80 years before it sank.

A reconstruction of the ship, Kyrenia II, sailed to Rhodes and back in 1982, loaded with a cargo of 30 tons.

Town and Harbour

Kyrenia was formerly enclosed within walls, fortified by towers, some of which remain today. The best preserved of these is located near the municipal market, on the high street. By following the direction of the curtain wall, other remnants may be identified: in particular, part of a tower retaining its machicolations may be seen to the left when passing from the market square along a side street running parallel to Canbulat Street. Towards the end of Canbulat Street, on the left hand side, opposite the Orthodox Archangelos church (now an icon museum) are the rock cut tombs, or catacombs, which date back to about 400 AD. Take a torch.

The harbour quay and mole are a product of British colonial times: in the middle ages the ships were simply drawn up on to the beach. On one of the buildings that line the harbour, a stone block with a hole for mounting a windlass can be observed. The entrance to the harbour was protected by a heavy chain which stretched from the present customs house to the tower on the opposite side. In the Lusignan period, the castle was served by an inner harbour, accessed by a large archway, now blocked up. This inner harbour, later filled in by the Venetians to form a dry moat, enabled communications with the outside world to be maintained in the event of the castle coming under seige.

In 1886 the British undertook extensive repairs and rebuilding of the harbour. An embankment and wharf had already been built on the south side, but the harbour was still shallow, and not protected from the north wind. A narrow gauge railway was laid between the harbour and a quarry to the west of the town, just below the small church of St.Barbara (now a mosque), to transport the stone. The project was completed in 1891, and the harbour assumed the shape which lasted until almost the end of the British occupation - a horseshoe shape open to the north, with moles to the east and west, a lighthouse being located on the western mole. However, there was still insufficient shelter from strong northern winds and storms, and a wall closing off the old harbour mouth was built in the middle of this century.

DETAIL OF MACHICOULIS ON TOWER IN CURTAIN-WALL

Folk Art Museum

In a little street just behind the harbour is the Folk Art Museum, which was established by Lady Loch.

On the upper floor, which is a reconstruction of Cypriot living quarters, bridal costumes, a variety of needlework, (including the famed Lefkara lace) and carved walnut bridal chests are on display. The most important item is a very rare medieval bronze plate. On the ground floor, the paraphernalia pertaining to peasant life can be seen, including an olive press, and a threshing board, made by securing flints into a large slab of wood.

Chrysokava

Between the small bay lying to the east of the castle, and the new harbour, where the ferries from Turkey dock, there is a rocky stretch of land on the seaward side of the jumble of houses and apartment blocks. Limestone blocks were quarried from here in ancient times, and the resulting architecture was utilized by early Christians who, unwelcome in the town, settled on the site. It is approached by turning left at the hospital, and after a couple of hundred yards, following a dirt road on the left which leads between blocks of flats down towards the sea. Entry is achieved by passing through the pair of iron gates set in the rocks.

Do not be deterred by the cylindrical water tanks just beyond the gates - the site is now used for growing vegetables. Remnants of a Roman aqueduct can be seen just inside the enclosure, and in the middle of the eastern rockface, a tunnel may be located, which leads into the next enclosure. To the right of the tunnel entrance is the rock cut chapel of Ayia Mavra, identified by the surviving fragments of its 10th century fresco. Christ is depicted sitting on a rainbow within an oval aureole, which is being transported to heaven by four angels. A row of apostles observe this event from the right hand side. Above the altar an isolated hand stretches up, its third finger delicately curved to touch the tip of the thumb. The style of the murals refers to Cappadocian wallpaintings of the 10th century in Turkey.

Passing through the tunnel, the principal feature in the next enclosure is the large cave, now used as an animal pen, and an extraordinary natural stone bridge.

SURROUNDINGS OF KYRENIA

BELLAPAIS ABBEY

Bellapais Abbey is by virtue of its situation and its architecture, one of the most beautiful monuments in Cyprus. A five minute taxi ride, or a 40 minute stroll will bring the visitor to the picturesque village of Bellapais perched on the mountainside about three miles east of Kyrenia.

History

The "Abbaye de la Paix", later corrupted to Bellapais, belonged to the Premonstratensian Order of Augustinian canons, and was founded under Archbishop Thierry in 1206. The Augustinian order fled from Palestine after the fall of Jerusalem in 1187, accompanied by white canons of the Order of St. Norbert, whose rule was adopted by the community in the abbey

Most of the abbey which survives today was built under the patronage of King Hugh III (1267-1284), who granted the Abbots the privilege of

45

wearing a bishop's mitre, and bearing gilded spurs and sword, when mounted. When Hugh III died in Tyre in 1284, his body was brought back to Cyprus and buried within the precincts of the abbey church.

The power and influence of the abbey during this period is implicit in the papal missives admonishing the abbey to submit to the authority of the Archbishop of Nicosia. Hugh IV (1324-1358) frequently retired to the abbey, where he added *'marvellous apartments'*.

Under the Venetians, the abbey fell into decline, and 16th century reports refer to dissolute morality, with many monks taking two or three wives. After the Osman conquest in 1571, the abbey was handed over to the orthodox church.

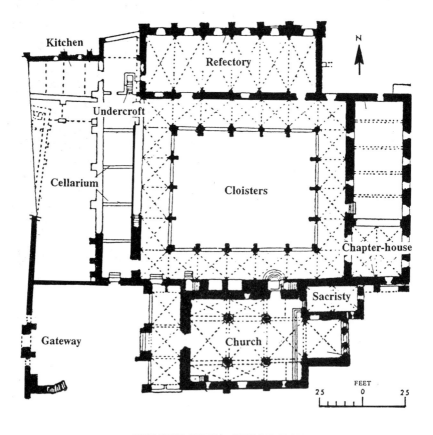

BELLAPAIS ABBEY - GROUND PLAN

THE LECTERN IN THE REFECTORY

Description

The first thing that strikes the visitor is the impressive fortified gateway, with its machicolated parapet, suggesting that it was sometimes necessary to defend the wealth of the abbey. A dry moat, now filled in, deterred entry other than over a drawbridge at the main gate.

Beyond the forecourt, the site of the former cellarium, are the cloisters, dating from the 14th century. Noteworthy features include the corbels, capitals and keystones decorated with foliage forms and heads of man and beast. Sadly, the magnificent tracery in the arcades has perished, with just a few stalks remaining. Nevertheless, the extant fragments indicate the flowing flamboyant style, suggestive of Spanish, rather than French influence. In the north west corner of the cloisters are two Roman sarcophagi at which the monks used to wash; the upper one, of elegantly

47

carved marble, is pierced by a row of holes which were formerly fitted with taps. All traces of the conduit which probably replenished this tank with water have vanished.

The marble lintel of the entrance to the adjacent refectory shows the arms of the Lusignans (right), the kings of Jerusalem (middle), and the kings of Cyprus and Jerusalem (left).

The refectory itself is a masterpiece of Gothic architecture with its sweeping ribbed vaulting intact after more than 700 years. The paved floor was removed long ago, and utilized in the surrounding village houses. The abbot's table was located on a dais at the eastern end of the hall, illumined through the circular window above, and an adjacent traceried window in the north wall. A further five windows pierce the north wall between the attached columns, in addition to smaller lights at the apex of the arches. The monks' benches were situated along the north and south walls, and traces of the supports are still clearly recognizable. A staircase built into the thickness of the north wall leads to the traceried lectern, where a reader would recite from edifying religious texts to the monks sitting silently below at their meal.

CARVED CORBELS IN THE CHAPTERHOUSE **(Camille Enlart)**

Behind the door in the west wall, which leads to the site of the former kitchen, a staircase passes down to the undercroft where provisions for the abbey were stored. Vaulting of trapezoidal section springs from simple corbels in the walls, and from the capitals of the row of octagonal pillars which divides the undercroft. Arrow slits in the north wall provide illumination, and a doorway from the eastern chamber opens on to a pathway leading up from the road.

In the southern section of the east wing is the chapter house where the monks sat on stone benches awaiting instructions from the abbot. The ceiling vaulting was supported by a central column of marble, probably originating from an early Christian basilica. Its massive springing stone lies nearby. The elaborately carved corbels in the walls reflect the imagination, and the high standard of workmanship of the Cypriot stonemasons at that period.

To the north of the chapter house lies the common room, the only room in the abbey which could be heated in winter. Mason marks may be seen on many of the stones which remain of this barrel vaulted chamber.

The dormitory was located in the upper storey of the east wing, and the wall cupboards where the monks used to keep their personal effects are visible from the commonroom below.

The church is the oldest part of the abbey, dating from the 13th century. Above the arched porch, which precedes the church, is a substantial belfry. On the south wall there are still traces to be seen of a 15th century painting in the Italian style. Cross-ribbed vaulting supports the roof of the nave and aisles in contrast to the barrel vaulting of the transept. In the north wall of the aisle, a staircase leads up to the dormitory, via a small room used for storing candles and lamps. The windows in the wall of the north aisle were blocked up when the cloisters were added. The simple, heavy architectural style of the church is reminiscent of contemporary structures in France and Germany.

Below the abbey to the north is a spring which issues from a long man made tunnel cut into the cliff on which the abbey stands. Nearby, an ancient road, known locally as the Crusader path, winds down to Ozanköy (Kazaphani). Some stretches of cobblestone survive.

The Necropolis of Vounous

Where the road from Kyrenia forks, with one branch leading up to Bellapais, the other branch leads to the village of Ozanköy. (Kazaphani) Following the road right through the village, pausing perhaps at the coffee shop (a focal point in any village) for refreshment, the tarmac surface eventually gives way to a dirt road leading to Çatalköy. (Ayios Epiktitos) After about half a mile, an isolated roadside house can be seen. A few yards before this house, a track peels off towards the right. Ignoring branches to the left, the track eventually comes to a dead end a few hundred yards from the road. To the right, and in fact all over the hillside, is the Bronze Age Necropolis of Vounous. The tombs have received the recent attention of treasure seekers, and mounds of freshly dug earth abound, along with scattered pot shards.

The numerous chamber tombs, hewn from the rock, have yielded a large variety of pots, jewellery, and also weapons and tools of bronze. Of particular significance are two terracotta models, one of oxen pulling the plough, and the other depicting a religious ritual scene. (These items are on display in the Cyprus Museum, in the Greek sector) Tomb finds such as these provide the major source of information of this period.

Hazreti Ömer Tekkesi

About three miles to the east of Kyrenia, a road leads to this important Islamic shrine, which is also a place of pilgrimage for Moslems.

During an Arab raid in the 7th century, an officer in Muawiya's army was killed, along with six of his men, and buried in a cave. After the Ottoman conquest, the dead, regarded as martyrs to Islam, were exhumed and reinterred. A shrine and mosque were erected over the graves.

Ayios Epiktitos Vrysi

A Neolithic settlement dating from between 4000 to 3000 BC was recently (1969) excavated in the north eastern corner of the 'Acapulco' holiday bungalows complex, about seven miles to the east of Kyrenia.

The settlement consists of a system of houses of varying plan, built partially underground, and connected together by narrow passages. The stone walls, which were up to two feet thick, were plastered on the inside. In each dwelling was a raised platform for the fireplace, next to which was a podium on which the occupants slept. Woven mats of plant fibre were used to cover the floor, and a reed thatch served for the roof. Bones of pigs, sheep, goats and cats were found between the houses. The dead were interred below the buildings. Items excavated by the archaeologists include stone axes, grinders, lamps, stone figurines, and a quantity of bone needles. In addition, a large number of pottery fragments were unearthed, of the type known as *Combed Ware* and *Red on White Ware*.

Continuing along the coast road towards Esentepe for a further nine miles, the turnoff to 16 mile beach may be recognized by a substantial stone sheep pen, terminated at its east end by a shepherds hut, or *mandra*. A rock cut tomb may be located in this vicinity by following the track to the left for about 100 yards, and then bearing right for a further 30 yards. It is easy to miss. A stepped *dromos* leads down to a carefully carved chamber which gives access to deep slots cut into the rock in three of its sides. Towards the sea are traces of a Roman settlement.

Five Finger Mountain

This 2400ft high massif is a readily identifiable feature of the Kyrenia Range, some seven miles to the east of the town. To the Turks it is known as Beşparmak; to the Greeks, Pentadaktylos. The origin of this mountain is the subject of many legends.

It is told that a certain queen, wishing to be rid of a young admirer, sent him off to fetch water from the spring of St.Andreas. Overcoming all the dangers and difficulties of the mission, the young man returned with a flask of the precious water. When the queen still refused to marry him, he emptied the flask onto the ground, took up a hand full of mud, and threw it at her. The muddy missile missed her and landed right where the mountain stands today.

Another version connects the mountain with the legendary Byzantine hero Dighenis, who leapt across to Cyprus from Asia Minor to escape from his Arab enemies. Grabbing the mountain as he pulled himself up, he left his handprint behind.

BUFFAVENTO

The main road east from Kyrenia follows the coast for about five miles, and then sweeps up to the mountains, crossing the range near the Five Finger peak. At the highest point in the pass, a rough road branches off to the west, leading to Buffavento Castle. This road recommends a 4 WD vehicle, or boots - a 90 minute march to base camp, plus 40 minutes for the final ascent. Take water and a snack with you.

The castle was built in Byzantine times, though its precise origin is obscure, and extended by the Lusignans. It had signal connections with St.Hilarion and Kantara, these three castles forming a defensive chain against Arab raids from without, and rebellion from within.

The first reports of the castle are in connection with Richard the Lionheart's conquest of Cyprus in 1191, and it is later reliably mentioned as the refuge in 1232 of Eschive of Montbeliard, the wife of Balian d'Ibelin, during the campaign against Emperor Frederick II.

51

Its inaccessible location defied both assault and escape, and it was sometimes used as a peacetime prison. In 1385, Perot and Glimot de Montolif were imprisoned there for conspiring against the Crown. Perot tried to escape by jumping from a balcony into a tree, but in doing so injured his leg, and was immediately recaptured. King James I pre-empted any further bids for liberty by decapitating both Perot, and his brother Glimot.

Sir John Visconti spent his last days in a dungeon at Buffavento castle, incarcerated there by King Peter I who construed Visconti's warning of the queen's infidelity as slander.

BUFFAVENTO CASTLE

Not much remains of the fortress which was abandoned in the 16th century. The nondescript collection of buildings beyond the entrance portal in the lower enciente, and those of the group higher up were mainly barracks and store rooms. Byzantine style brickwork may be seen in the door and window arches of some chambers in the upper castle. Defensive structures were rendered unnecessary by the surrounding sheer drops.

Van Bruyn recorded his visit to Buffavento in 1683:

'The ascent is as difficult and dangerous as I have ever made. The greater part of the time we had to climb with our hands as well as our feet, and whichever way we turned our gaze we saw only what made our hair stand on end. We took an hour and a half to reach the top'.

When the Venetians took control of Cyprus, they concentrated their attention on fortifying Kyrenia, Nicosia, and Famagusta; Buffavento was partially dismantled.

The upper castle of Buffavento - 'Defier of Winds'- is 3000ft above sea level, and affords spectacular views along the coast and across the interior of the island.

Ayios Chrysostomos Monastery

Lying to the south of Buffavento, the 'White Monastery' once formed part of the See of the Patriarch of Jerusalem.

The main church of St. Chrysostomos, built in the 11th century, was of the eight column type. (see Antiphonitis below) It was torn down at the beginning of this century and replaced by a new building.

The neighbouring church of Ayia Trias was built by the Byzantine governor Philokales Evmathios. Inscriptions and frescoes dating from the 12th century were restored in 1963 by the "Dumbarton Oaks Byzantine Institute". The monastery is not open to the public at present.

Sourp Magar

Returning from Buffavento to the Five Finger pass, the main road can be crossed, and a forestry road followed to the east. After about five miles, the Sourp Magar Monastery may be seen in the valley below, to the left. This monastery belonged originally to a small Coptic Christian community, who dedicated it to St.Magar (309-404). It is best accessed from the picnic area located a mile or so further along the road.

In the 15th century the monastery passed into Armenian possession, and became a famous place of pilgrimage for Armenians on their way to and from the Holy Land. After the Armenian pogroms in Turkey at the end of the 19th century, an orphanage was set up in Nicosia which used the monastery as its summer seat. The present ruins date from the beginning of the 19th century.

Two hundred yards beyond the picnic area the forestry track joins a tarmac road, which, turning left, leads down to Esentepe (Ayios Amvrosios), and is an alternative approach to the Antiphonitis Monastery. (see below)

Antiphonitis Church

The tarmac road through Esentepe (Ayios Amvrosios) winds towards the mountains, and quite soon after leaving the village, a dirt road branches off to the left where the tarmac road curves sharply to the right. The dirt road passes along the wooded hillsides for three or four miles and arrives at a fork, identified by a short square column. The branch to the left leads to a picturesque valley, which is the site of the monastery church of St.Antiphonitis.

The dome of this 12th century church rests on eight round stone columns, arranged in an irregular octogon. Two of the columns, detached from the walls, mark the division between the altar and the main body of the church. It is in fact the sole surviving example of this type of structure in Cyprus. The barrel vaulted narthex and the arcade to the south of the church are 15th century Frankish additions. This arcade, or loggia, built of medium grain limestone, is an exquisite example of Gothic workmanship. It once had a roof of wood and clay, and a stone balustrade between the arches.

Many of the frescoes which adorned the walls inside the church have been destroyed or removed in recent years by art robbers, but some remain. The paintings within the sanctuary, and those in the south west sector of the nave date from the end of the 12th century, and are in the late Comnenian style of the Byzantine capital, Constantinople.

In the conch of the apse, the Virgin Mary is depicted flanked by the Archangels Gabriel and Michael. Mary is portrayed in the Blachernitissa mode, with Christ represented within a medallion. The faces of the Virgin and Gabriel are missing, but enough of Michael's face remains to reveal the artist as a remarkable precursor of the much later renaissance style in Italy. The Archangels are clothed in the costume of ushers to the Byzantine court. Michael is represented again, holding a parchment script, on the upper section of the detached north column; Gabriel mirrors him on the south detached column. Below Gabriel is a geometric design with a pair of partridges in a centre circle.

Most of the mural on the south west wall of the nave is missing, except for the blue hooded figure of St.Anthony, but the Baptism of Christ, on the upper part of the column to the left, is well preserved. As he walks across the river Jordan, Christ blesses the personification of the river, and is baptized by John the Baptist. On the lower half of the column is the figure of St. Endoxus, and to the left, that of St. Paul. A few traces of the transfiguration remain on the ceiling of the south west corner.

VIEW OF ANTIPHONITIS MONASTERY CHURCH

The other frescoes date from the 15th century. The depiction of the Last Judgement above the north entrance to the nave has been all but removed: a headless Christ enthroned in an oval iridescent aureole, and a few figures on the adjoining columns, are all that remain. However, a most interesting painting of the birth of the Virgin Mary is well preserved on the upper section of the column to the left, facing west. The theme is drawn from the apocryphal gospels, and shows St.Anna lying on a wooden bed with the infant Mary in an open box at the foot of the bed. The contrast between the renaissance palace in the background, which is drawn in perspective, and the deliberately out of perspective bed and box, with the icon like figure of Mary, is significant. Divine images were

55

often portrayed in an unreal way, to emphasise their other-worldliness. Furthermore, the unusual combination of Byzantine and renaissance elements enables this picture to be placed at the end of the 15th century. On the lower half of the same column is an image of St.Peter, facing St.Paul on the opposite column.

Of the Tree of Jesse, on the south wall, only the legs of Jesse, and a mounted figure (the prophet Balaam) at the bottom left hand side have escaped the private collector. The tree, sprouting from Jesse's body, is supposed to represent the genealogical descent of Christ, with various ancestors dotted about the branches, and the Virgin Mary with Christ at the summit. The column on the right portrays the well preserved image of St. Romanus, a Byzantine hymn writer.

The frescoes in the dome have remained out of reach to vandal and robber alike, and though incomplete, they have not suffered the indignity of incised graffiti. Christ Pantocrator is shown inside a medallion surrounded by angels approaching the Throne, which is flanked by the Virgin Mary and John the Baptist. The annulus beyond depicts the twelve apostles seated on their thrones, and in a further annulus, in the drum of the dome, are painted the images of the prophets, in pairs between the windows.

Outside the church, a clump of trees may be seen when looking north west from the boundary wall, some twenty feet away. The *Liquid Amber* tree has maple shaped leaves which are held to possess aphrodisial properties. An extract from the bark is supposed to be effective against lice, and the monks used to burn the wood as incense.

Panayia Melandryna Monastery

Regaining the coast road via Esentepe, impressive stone carob warehouses may be seen on the seashore. Two miles beyond the junction, a track leads off to the right just after a small bridge. There is vehicular access to within a stone's throw of the overgrown monastery church of Melandryna, set amongst fig trees and the remnants of a citrus orchard. This barrel vaulted 15th century structure was reinforced in the 18th century by the addition of substantial flying buttresses. A noteworthy feature is the use of double arches in the portals, a medieval method of strengthening the doorways. Inside the church only a fragment of the 16th century iconostasis remains, showing a floral design with gilt details on a blue background.

To the west of the church is evidence of earlier occupation of this site: foundation walls and pillar drums may be seen in addition to potshards (some glazed), and several rock cut shaft tombs. To the north of the church is a well. The original capstone, carved from solid rock, lies broken in two, its place usurped by a crude botch of concrete and iron.

Panayia Pergaminiotissa

Eight miles further east, the turnoff to Geçitkale (Lefkoniko) is signposted. This road traverses the mountains in a delightful winding pass of the type which once linked Kyrenia to the Mesaoria.

Continuing along the coast road, a T - junction is reached. To the right lies Tatlısu (Akanthou). Turning left, the road passes a large cistern on the right hand side built from large stone blocks, which are probably the only remains of the ancient city of Aphrodisium. The road soon bears right, and three miles further on, a hillock on the right hand side announces the site of a Hellenistic and Roman settlement, to the south of which lies the church of Panayia Pergaminiotissa.

On top of the hillock, where the acropolis of this Hellenistic town was located, may be seen a large stone pillar drum, part of a stone basin and some foundation walls. Towards the western side, a small patch of pebble mosaic flooring is revealed. Further west is an unusual rock cut tomb which was later used as a chapel. Note the curious plumbing arrangements nearby. Shaft tombs cut into the rock may be seen in this area, which was the necropolis of the town. To the south of the hillock is a well with the footholds for descending and ascending gouged into the rock walls. Other wells, or cisterns, are located close by.

The 12th century domed church of Panayia Pergaminiotissa, further to the south, is built on the site of an early Christian basilica, the foundations of which are easily recognized. In particular the triple apse of the earlier structure is clearly discernible amongst the jumble of pillar drums and capitals which lie strewn about. Inside the church are fragments of Franco-byzantine murals, now inaccessible since the entrances have been blocked up. To the south of the church is a large, bottle shaped water cistern.

On the left hand side a mile further to the east can be seen the small barrel vaulted church of Ayios Kharalambos, which was evidently built on the remains of a former mill. Square section buttresses at each corner of the church counter the vaulting thrust, and the demi-hemisphere roof of the apse is supported by a polygonal choir. Inside is a rare stone iconostasis which probably predates the 15th century church. The field behind is littered with potshards.

Hogarth's tomb

The coast road continues eastwards, passing more carob warehouses, and the junction to Mersinlik (Phlamoudi). A mile and a half past this junction, opposite a small sandy bay, a rough track leads inland. About a quarter of a mile up the track, following the third path to the left for some fifty yards, a large tomb cut into the rock below ground level may be discovered. Doric columns carved from the rock are a notable feature which are also present in some of the 'Tombs of the Kings' in Paphos. Similar peristyle tombs dating from Hellenistic times have been found in Egypt and Macedonia. Crosses carved into the rock may have served to exorcize pagan spirits, or may indicate subsequent use in Christian times. The tomb was probably the last resting place of a local dignitary or Ptolemaic official.

CAROB WAREHOUSES ON THE NORTH COAST

ST.HILARION CASTLE

Shortly before the highway threading the Kyrenia pass dives down into the Mesaoria, a signpost indicates the road which winds and climbs up the mountain until it enters the alpine valley at the foot of the castle.

ST. HILARION CASTLE - A VIEW FROM THE SOUTH

History

This spectacular mountain castle takes its name not from St.Hilarion the Great, who died near Paphos in the 4th century, but from a later hermit monk of the same name who, seeking peace and seclusion, lived out his days in a cave nearby. In the 10th. century, the Byzantines built a monastery here in his memory. This was later converted into the castle, known as Didymos (twins) from the twin peaks crowning the mountain.

St.Hilarion, along with Buffavento and Kantara, served as watch towers to give warning of approaching saracen pirates. The castle is mentioned in accounts of Richard the Lionheart's conquest of the island on his way to Palestine in 1191, during the third crusade.

In 1227, Jean d'Ibelin, Lord of Beirut, became bailli of Cyprus for the minority of King Henry I. It was known that Emperor Frederick II, who was suzerain of Cyprus, was preparing for a crusade to Palestine. Jean

59

d'Ibelin, anticipating difficulties, fortified and extended St.Hilarion, then known as Dieu d'Amour, as a safe retreat. Frederick arrived at Limassol in 1228, and after quarrelling with d'Ibelin, continued with him to Palestine, leaving Henry, and Cyprus, in the charge of Amalric Barlais and four other baillis. After Frederick's return to Europe, Barlais confiscated Ibelin property. Jean d'Ibelin returned to Cyprus in force and defeated Barlais, who fled to Dieu d'Amour, taking with him King Henry. The castle was starved into surrender in 1230, and d'Ibelin took over the government pending Henry's majority. In 1231, Frederick sent forces which besieged d'Ibelins castle at Beirut. Jean d'Ibelin and King Henry set sail with an army to relieve the city whereupon Barlais, aided by Frederick's troops, overran the island, and besieged Henry's sisters in Dieu d'Amour. Jean d'Ibelin and Henry returned just in time to relieve the starving castle, and by 1233, the remnants of Frederick's forces had been driven from Cyprus.

In subsequent years St.Hilarion became the summer residence of the Lusignans where noble ladies could watch from the ramparts as the knights jousted on the mountain meadows below.

The Venetians, who took over the island in 1489, relied on the fortresses of Kyrenia, Famagusta, and Nicosia for their defences, and partially dismantled St.Hilarion, leaving its ruins as a source of romantic inspiration.

Description

St.Hilarion was divided into three levels, or encientes, each with its own supplies of water, provisions, and weapons.

Entering the gatehouse and passing through the bailey, the restored portal with its fine carved corbels leads into the lower castle. This compound used to accommodate the troops and horses. The ruined stalls and the water cisterns, which still retain the winter rains, can be seen. The path follows the old Byzantine walls, which are reinforced at intervals by horseshoe towers, and then turns up towards the gateway of the middle castle. This entrance was fitted with a drawbridge in Frankish times. A vaulted passageway leads into the knights' residential area.

Steps lead up to the Byzantine church, which dates from the 10th century. Its cupola rests on eight round masonry columns, arranged as an irregular octogon, a style which survives elsewhere in Cyprus only at the Antiphonitis monastery (see page 54). The Byzantine building

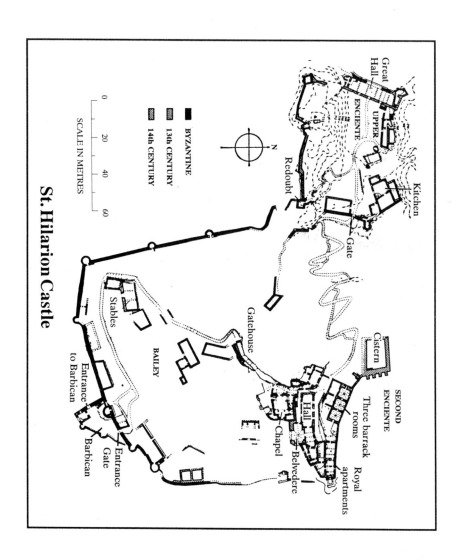

ST. HILARION CASTLE - GROUND PLAN

technique is revealed in the alternating layers of stone and brick. Next to the church is a small sacristy. North of the church, steps lead down to a vaulted passage, which opens on to a lookout place, or 'belvedere'. This offers excellent views along the north slopes of the Kyrenia range.

Behind the passage lies a large hall, the refectory where the knights dined, and where the visitor too may take refreshment before his assault on the upper castle. Around the refectory are grouped further buildings: a kitchen area with larders, the remains of a four storey living quarters, and several barracks. Beyond the barracks is a massive buttressed water tank: water supplies for the castle were obtained by collecting the winter rains, which were channelled into large cisterns.

THE 'QUEEN'S WINDOW' IN THE UPPER CASTLE **(Camille Enlart)**

A steep, windy path leads up to the upper castle which is entered through a gateway in the wall. Note the hinge sockets, and the deep slot in the thickness of the wall on the left, from which the beam barring the door was drawn. To the right are the remains of a group of service buildings, including a kitchen. Following the path to the west, past two cisterns, the royal palace can be found, wedged between two great crags, 730m above the sea. On the second storey of this building is the "Queens Window": through the Gothic tracery the village of Karaman (Karmi) can be seen nestling against the mountainside. A view to the right, beyond the royal apartments, reveals the practical, if primitive, toilet facilities.

Before leaving the upper castle, it is worth climbing up (more steps!) to the tower of the Prince of Antioch, who is supposed to have plunged his Bulgarian bodyguard into the abyss in a fit of rage.

A forest road continues on towards the west from St.Hilarion coming out at Lapta (Lapithos) and at Karşıyaka (Vasilia). This trip is highly recommended, offering spectacular views to either side of the range.

Necropolis of Karmi

At Karaoğlanoğlu (Ayios Yeoryios), which lies to the west of Kyrenia, the road branches towards the mountains, passing through Edremit, and continuing on to the holiday village of Karaman (Karmi). Shortly before reaching Karaman, a track leads off to the left, to the necropolis, which dates from the Middle Bronze Age (1850-1050 BC). This site, which was excavated in 1961 by the Australian archaeologist James Stewart, is in some respects one of the most interesting and significant Bronze Age burial grounds in Cyprus. In contrast to earlier tomb structures, a number of burial chambers are grouped around the dromos, or access passage. Carved on the wall of one dromos is a female figure whose prominent reproductive organs suggest that she is a fertility goddess, a deity borrowed from oriental mythology, who may be interpreted as symbolizing the rebirth expected by those interred. The presence of the goddess, and the pilasters carved into the dromos walls and tomb entrance, alludes to coeval temenos architecture; this feature is unique in Cyprus. In another grave, blue faience beads from Egypt, and a Minoan Kamares cup were found; these represent the first evidence of trading relations with Egypt and Crete.

Lambousa / Ancient Lapithos

The ancient and early Byzantine town of Lambousa lies about ten miles west of Kyrenia, and is reached by taking the second turning to the right past the turn off to Mare Monte Hotel. This road leads into a restricted military area, but soon bears off to the right, passing a huge isolated block of rock on the left hand side, to a parking area behind the military restaurant Mücahit Aile Gazinosu. It is regretted that inspection of this interesting site is limited to what is visible from the immediate vicinity of the restaurant. Photographs are not permitted.

Lambousa was founded in the 8th century BC and coin finds indicate that this site, an important city kingdom in ancient times, was in the hands of the Phoenicians in the 5th & 4th centuries BC. It remained a flourishing port in Roman and Byzantine times, until it was destroyed by fire during the Arab raids in 647. Below the hill, where the acropolis once stood, are Roman rooms, hewn from the living rock. In these rooms, fused mosaic fragments were discovered, evidence of the town's cremation. The harbour of the ancient town was situated below the restaurant, and further to the east are Roman fishtanks, connected to the sea via inlet and outlet channels.

Pococke recorded his visit in 1728:

'We set forward towards the west, and travelled about two leagues to the ruins of antient Lapithos, which I suppose to be the capital of another kingdom Here, I saw several walls that were cut out of the rock, and one entire room over the sea; there are also remains of some towers and walls, but the old name is translated to a village near called Lapta, where there are some sources of very fine water, which seem to be those of the antient river Lapithos. I lay here at the rich convent called Acropede'.

To the west of the restaurant near the shore is the beautiful little Franco-Byzantine church of St.Evlalios, referred to by Strambaldi in 1458. Further west stands the Monastery of Acheiropietos ('not hand made'). The 14th century church was built on the ruins of an early Byzantine predecessor, whose apse was incorporated into the new structure. The curious name of the monastery derives from the legend which relates that the building was rescued from heathen violation by the Virgin, who transferred it overnight from Asia Minor to its present location. Another legend tells that the Turin Shroud was once kept here. Carved into the block of rock referred to above is the chapel of St.Evlambios. Silver plate discovered in Lambousa bears the earliest known hallmarks.

Lapta (Lapithos)

The Arab raids on the coastal town of Lambousa during the 7th century persuaded the inhabitants to relocate their town further inland, and resulted in the founding of Lapithos, a few miles to the south west of Lambousa.

In fact settlements existed in this area since Neolithic times: Gjerstad excavated several round huts of a Chalcolithic colony, and recent metallurgical analyses of finds in this district reveal early exploitation of the local copper deposits. In one of the numerous Iron Age chamber tombs, skeletal remains suggest that slaves accompanied their masters into the next world.

In medieval times the population of Lapithos rose to 10,000, its importance stemming from its perpetual springs which irrigated the surrounding citrus orchards, and powered the flour mills. Pottery was manufactured in large quantities and exported.

Pottery is still made in the village, now known as Lapta, and the lemon groves are still watered by the Başpinar springs which issue from the mountain side high above. The forestry road which runs from St. Hilarion to Karşıyaka may be accessed from Lapta by following the winding road up through the village aided by the occasional sign indicating the location of the *Başpinar Restaurant.* Beyond the restaurant (which serves good local food) the road ascends the mountain to the ridge where it joins the forestry road. This junction offers good views across the Mesaoria plain to the Troodos mountains in the south.

NICOSIA / LEFKOŞA

Nicosia, the divided capital of Cyprus, lies in the Mesaoria, the central plain stretching along the island between the Kyrenia range and the Troodos mountains.

History

The ancient city kingdom of Ledra, with its sanctuary to Aphrodite, is mentioned in various Greek inscriptions dating from the 4th century BC.

Lefkos, son of Ptolemy Soter, rebuilt the city in about 300 BC, and his name is perpetuated in the local name for Nicosia, Lefkoşa.

In Byzantine times the city sustained an influx of people, who may have come from the coastal towns, seeking the security of the interior to avoid the rapacity of arab pirates. However, Nicosia did not play a significant role in the history of Cyprus until the advent of the crusaders.

Richard the Lionheart conquered the island in 1191, on his way to Palestine during the third crusade, and subsequently sold it to the Knights Templar. These knights rapidly made themselves unpopular, and in 1192 a popular uprising in Nicosia drove them into their stronghold in the city.

In the same year Richard permitted Guy de Lusignan, who had lost his kingdom of Jerusalem, to buy the government of Cyprus from the Templars, and from that time onwards, Nicosia remained the capital city of the island.

Nicosia flourished under the Lusignans, combining European art with Oriental luxury. Magnificent palaces and churches were built, as well as fine town houses. This glittering period in the history of the city ended with the invasion of the Mamelukes in 1426, when the city was plundered, and the palaces burnt down.

In 1489 the Venetians took over the island and it capital. Anticipating Ottoman ambitions towards Cyprus, the Venetians took steps to fortify its towns. In 1567 the Italian military engineer Giulio Savorgnano was commissioned to rebuild the defenses of Nicosia according to the latest methods. As a result, huge earthworks were thrown up around a much reduced city centre. Eleven mighty bastions were spaced around the

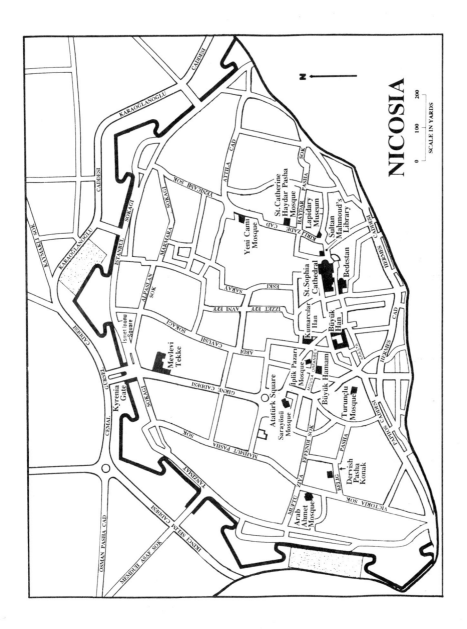

perimeter, and the whole work was clad in stone. A dry moat encircled the walls, and the city beyond was razed to provide an open range for the artillery. During this operation, most of the churches and palaces, including the Dominican Monastery, the last resting place of the Lusignans, were destroyed.

Notwithstanding these preparations, Nicosia fell to the forces of Lala Mustapha Pasha after a seven week seige in 1570. As the city was taken by storm, the beseigers were allowed three days of plundering, during which 20,000 of the inhabitants were massacred.

For the next three hundred years, Nicosia gradually deteriorated and by the time the British took over in 1878, the city was a squalid shadow of itself, with its fine buildings tumbling in ruin.

Under the British, many public works were undertaken: roads were built, utilities were installed, and by the time Cyprus became an independent republic in 1960, Nicosia was well on the way to becoming a modern European city.

Kyrenia Gate

Nicosia within the walls can be entered through the Kyrenia gate, known formerly as "Porta Del Proveditore" after the Proveditore Francesco Barbaro. Above the gate on the inside is a marble panel inscribed in Latin, recording 1562 as the date of construction. The monogram of Sultan Mahmoud II on another plaque marks the restoration of the gate in 1821. On the outer side of the gate, an inset panel records the following verse, in Arabic script,

"O Mohammed, give these tidings to the faithful: victory is from God, and triumph is near. O opener of doors, open for us the best of all doors."

In 1931 the British built roads on either side of the Kyrenia gate to accommodate motor traffic.

Mevlevi Tekke

A few paces from the Kyrenia gate is the Tekke, or monastery, of the whirling dervishes, an order founded by the poet and mystic Jelal-ed-din Roumi Mevlana in the 13th century.

Monastic orders were banned by Kemal Atatürk in 1925, and the domed building, dating from the 17th century, now serves as a museum for Turkish arts and craft.

Central to the religious life of the Mevlana Order is the ritual dance. Music was played, a reed flute playing a prominent role, and the dervishes whirled themselves into ecstacy; with one palm facing up to heaven, and the other facing downwards to the earth they symbolized mankind as being the bridge between the earthly and heavenly spheres.

Adjoining the central hall, where the dancing took place, is a long corridor containing the tombs of the sheikhs who ruled the order in Cyprus. Ottoman gravestones and remains of Roman columns can be seen in the garden.

Atatürk Square and the Venetian Column

In the middle of the square stands a twenty foot granite column erected by the Venetians as a symbol of their rule. It was torn down and cast aside during the Turkish conquest, but re-erected by the British early this century. Capping the column is a copper globe which replaces the original lost lion of St.Mark. Around the base can be seen coats-of-arms of noble Venetian families.

On the north side of the square stands an administrative building in typical British colonial style. This was the site of the former Venetian governors palace, and the seat of the later Turkish governors. The palace was demolished in 1904 by the British, but various items of architectural interest were recovered and can be seen in the lapidary museum.

A good view across the divided city can be obtained from the roof of the Saray Hotel. Behind this hotel stands the Sarayönü mosque, built in 1902 by a British architect who drew on several disparate elements of Islamic style to create this unique structure.

Dervish Pasha Konak

This 19th century mansion, standing in the old quarter of Arab Ahmet, was restored in 1988, and opened to the public as a Folklore museum. The former owner, Dervish Pasha, was the publisher of the first turkish newspaper in Cyprus.

The ground floor, built of stone and surrounded by arcades, provided accommodation for the servants. The first floor, made of mud bricks, comprised bedrooms, womens quarters, baths, a kitchen, and the architecturally exceptional reception hall, or *selamlık.*

This hall, the most important room in a turkish house, was where guests were received. There are benches along three walls of the room, known as *sedir* in Turkish.

Arab Ahmet Mosque

This mosque, and the quarter in which it stands, is named after the Turkish governor Arab Ahmet. It was built in 1845 on the site of a former church, and is a fine specimen of later Turkish architecture. The large dome, 50 ft across, rests on four arcaded arches, and the entrance porch, facing north, is capped with three small domes. In the garden are gravestones of Turkish governors and Turkish-Cypriot statesmen.

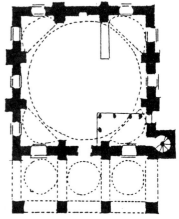

ARAB AHMET MOSQUE

Turunçlu Mosque

This mosque, which lies in the İplik Pazarı quarter (cotton market), was built in 1825 by the Ottoman governor Seyit Mehmet Aga. The building resembles a 19th century Cypriot church, with its buttresses and arcaded porches. The wooden roof rests on four broad arches supported by wooden columns with decorated capitals. Note the ornamented Mecca niche, and the marble pulpit.

İplik Pazarı Mosque

This 19th century mosque takes its name from its proximity to the old cotton market which existed here in crusader and Ottoman times. The minaret, with its knot shaped pinnacle, stems from a former structure, on the site of which this mosque was erected.

The fine finish of the stone walls is a testament to the skills of the contemporary stonemasons.

70

Büyük Hamam

The history of this building is somewhat uncertain. It was supposed to have been the church St.George of the Latins, later converted into a turkish bath, but there are architectural inconsistancies, suggesting that the Gothic portal may have come from another site. The turkish baths housed in this building still function, and are open to the public.

Büyük Han

Close by to the Büyük Hamam are the two caravanserais, or inns, Büyük Han and Kumarcılar Han.

The Büyük Han, or Great Inn, was built after the Ottoman conquest by the first governor, Muzaffer Pasha, from the ruins of an old Frankish building, in 1572. It follows the standard pattern of Anatolian inns, and in terms of architecture and cultural history, it is the most important relic of the Ottoman period in Cyprus.

The caravanserais and city inns served to accommodate travellers, but were also commercial centres, comparable to the Italian Fondacchi, where goods were stored and exchanged.

OCTAGONAL MOSQUE IN THE COURTYARD
OF THE BÜYÜK HAN

The rooms are arranged in two stories around a rectangular courtyard with beautiful vaulted arcades forming verandahs. The ground floor was reserved for shops, storage rooms, and chambers for business transactions. Lodging was provided on the upper floor, where the rooms were fitted with carpets and fireplaces. (Note the elegant carved chimneys

71

projecting in a row above the roof.) The stables were located outside the inn. In the middle of the courtyard a small domed mosque is raised on an octagonal arcade; below, a tank supplies water for ablution.

During the British colonial period, the Büyük Han was used as a prison. It is now undergoing extensive renovation.

Kumarcılar Han

A short distance to the north east of Büyük Han lies the Kumarcilar Han, or *gamblers inn*. Today it houses the Department of Antiquities. A portal in the entrance passage which leads to the courtyard exhibits Gothic details, suggesting that the inn was built on an earlier structure. Arcades form galleries which give access to the rooms in this two storey building.

ST.SOPHIA CATHEDRAL (Selimiye Mosque)

Situated in the middle of Nicosia, next to the market, this fine building still dominates the capital, and its towering minarets are a feature of the city skyline.

History

The foundation stone of this cathedral was laid in 1209 during the incumbency of the latin Archbishop Thierry, but the realization of the project was the result of the architectural ambitions of Archbishop Eustorge de Montaigu (1217-1250). His aspirations led to the complaint by the papal legate Eudes de Chateauroux, that the income of the diocese was spent almost exclusively on building the cathedral.

King Louis IX of France, who sojourned in Cyprus during the 7th crusade, and who had with him many artisans and engineers, supplied the final impetus to the construction program. Indeed, it is not inconceivable that Eude de Montruil, one of the master builders of Saint Denis, had a hand in the building of St.Sophia. However, it was not until 1326 that the cathedral was finally completed and consecrated.

The building suffered severe damage during the invasions of the Genoese in 1373, and the Mamelukes in 1426. Repairs were evidently made by the time John II was crowned king of Cyprus in the cathedral in 1432.

WEST FRONT OF ST. SOPHIA (Sydney Vacher)

When the Venetians took over the island, they also appropriated the church treasure. Further damage occurred during the earthquakes of 1491 and 1547.

The last Christian service was conducted by Francesco Contarini, the Bishop of Paphos, a few days before the Ottoman conquest in 1570. The cathedral was subsequently converted into a mosque; the glass windows were removed, and the interior was stripped of its decoration, and then whitewashed. The following year minarets were added, and a mihrab placed inside to indicate the the direction of Mecca to the faithful.

In 1954 the mosque was renamed Selimiye mosque in memory of Sultan Selim II, whose armies conquered the island.

Description

St.Sophia, one of the most imposing Gothic structures in the Levant, takes its name from an earlier Byzantine building which existed on the same site. (Greek Ayia Sophia means divine wisdom)

Above the splendid entrance porch in the western facade is a magnificent traceried window, flanked by two towers, which have been converted into minarets. The porch itself is a massive structure in three sections, matching the three entrances to the nave and the aisles, and is

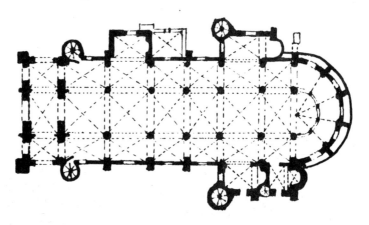

ST. SOPHIA CATHEDRAL - PLAN

a 14th century addition to the cathedral. The mouldings of the marble entrance portals are profusely decorated in deep relief with four leaved flower motifs, and other foliage designs. In addition, small figurines, possibly of saints, adorn the arch of the nave portal. Whilst identical in form to each other, the aisle entrances display quite different details of decoration, as a passing glance will reveal.

The interior of the cathedral is divided by two rows of six massive columns which are linked in the apse by four granite columns (reportedly from Salamis) with early Byzantine and Gothic capitals, arranged in a semicircle. The somewhat squat style of Gothic architecture in Cyprus (note the absence of a triforium) is a precaution against earthquakes. A notable feature is the bare, raised gallery, built on the thickness of the wall along either side of the aisles, and accessed by small staircases immediately to the right and left of the aisle entrances. This arrangement was used in Burgundian churches in the 13th century and in those of the Champagne. It is no coincidence that the wife of the Lusignan king, Hugh I (1205-18) was the energetic and enterprising Alice of Champagne. The earlier parts of the cathedral - the ambulatory and transept - show other elements of Champagne influence, in the profiles of the cornices and corbels.

The apsidial chapels, adjoining the transept on each side, follow a Palestinian pattern, and likewise, the style of Outremer is evident in the frieze and capitals of the north transept entrance portal. The chapel in the north transept was consecrated to St.Nicolas. From here a staircase leads to the Moslem ladies' gallery, which connects to the former treasure chamber of the cathedral via some narrow steps. In the southern transept, where the *mihrab* now stands, was a chapel of the

EASTERN VIEW OF ST. SOPHIA

Virgin Mary. The chapel next to it, where there are some gravestones from the middle ages, was dedicated to St.Thomas Aquinas, who had dedicated his work *"The Guidance of Princes"* to King Hugh III of Cyprus.

The Bedestan

On the south side of St.Sophia cathedral stands the former Orthodox Metropolis, which was converted into a market, or Bedestan during the Ottoman conquest.

This hybrid structure, which combines Byzantine, Gothic and renaissance elements, consists of two southern aisles of 12th century origin, and a nave and north aisle dating from the 15th century. The nave is domed at the transept, and the apse is delicately vaulted, with six ribs converging at the keystone high above. There is no evidence of galleries or a triforium, and in general, the structure is quite plain, with decoration limited to the capitals.

BEDESTAN - A VIEW FROM THE SOUTHWEST

At the eastern end of the nave, an earlier entrance is blocked off, and three portals have been inserted into the north wall. These are finely carved, though less elaborate and much smaller than those of neighbouring St.Sophia. The middle door has a sculptured relief of the death of the virgin Mary carved on its marble lintel.

On the southside of the church is a small museum, two small chambers containing assorted incised and inscribed stone slabs, and a few amphorae. The second chamber has a remarkable ceiling, constructed by the Ottomans, consisting of wooden planks decorated by wooden beading nailed on to form a vast matrix of squares with triangulated corners.

BEDESTAN - NORTH PORTAL   FLAMBOYANT TRACERY WINDOW

Sultan Mahmud's Library

Situated opposite the eastern end of St.Sophia, this domed building was founded in 1829 by Sultan Mahmud II, who supplied some books from his own collection. The library also houses some rare Arabic, Turkish and Persian manuscripts.

Lapidary Museum (Jefferey's Museum)

Close by is the Lapidary Museum, a restored Venetian building which houses a collection of stone articles including coats of arms, sarcophagi, marble panels and column segments. Opposite the entance door is a beautiful tracery window, in the flamboyant style which came from the old governors palace, now demolished.

Worthy of note is the carved sarcophagus of the Dampierre family, and the gravestone of Adam of Antioch, who was Marshall of Cyprus in the 13th century.

CHURCH OF ST.CATHERINE (Haydar Pasha Mosque)

The history of this 14th century Gothic church, located just a stones throw from the Lapidary Museum, is largely unknown. After the Ottoman conquest, this latin church was converted into a mosque. This involved the removal of the glass windows, carved decorations and church furniture and equipment, followed by the installation of minarets, a mihrab and a mimber.

Description

The external walls are arranged with trapezoidal buttresses alternating with tall narrow windows, which are divided by slender mullions. The window space has been filled with 'Doyly lights', slabs of gypsum perforated with geometric designs. Dripstones run all the way around the church, above and below the windows. Access to the nave is through the ornate gothic south portal. The hood of this entrance, deeply carved with foliage designs, and capped with a finial, is supported on corbels which have been defaced, probably because they were carved with figures. The arch and lintel of the doorway rest on carved capitals supported by

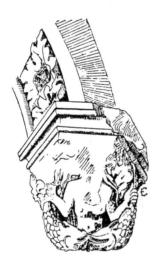

a triple columned door jamb. The detached middle column is made of white marble. Above the lintel, which bears the three Lusignan shields (now completely obliterated), the tympanum is filled with blind tracery.

The larger western entrance is similar in design, but more finely executed, a good example of the *Flamboyant* style in Cyprus. Springing from the hood corbels are two decorated pinnacles, but the finial above the arch is missing. The lintel is carved with a frieze of dragons and roses.

The small doorway in the north wall led to cloisters, and is plainer in design, only the inner surface of the hood being carved. However, the corbels are interesting, one depicting a dragon, and the other a naked woman holding two fish by their tails. The cusps of the quatrefoil tracery in the tympanum terminate in fleurs-de-lis.

Inside, there are no side aisles, and the cross ribbed vaulting is supported on elaborately carved capitals of moulded pillars which are built into the wall. Steel ties span the church high up, inserted to counteract the lateral thrust exerted by the vaulting, which had caused the walls to bulge. The nave is terminated by a polygonal choir. To the left of the choir is a small sacristy, whose 'spider' vaulting rests on corbels, one carved as a human face, the others with foliage. A double

HAYDAR PASHA MOSQUE - WEST PORTAL

flower adorns the keystone of this vaulting, and is repeated in the main body of the church. Above the sacristy is another chamber, possibly the treasury, with a window looking into the church. It is possible that a holy relic was once displayed there. A font on the right hand side of the choir once drained through the wall, and flowed from a spout, which may be seen in the tiny chamber accessed from the east end of the church through a small archway.

On the left hand side, just inside the entrance, is a staircase leading to the minaret.

The church of St.Catherine is an excellent and complete example of French Gothic architecture at the end of the 14th century.

GÜZELYURT (Morphou)

The road west from Kyrenia follows the coast until a few miles past Lapta (Lapithos), when it turns inland, passing Çamlıbel (Myrtou) and Tepebaşı (Dhiorios) before descending to the plains of Güzelyurt.

St.Mamas Monastery

This monastery, and also the museum, are located near the new mosque which can be found without difficulty.

According to one of the legends which have sprung up around this saint, the hermit Mamas is supposed to have stubbornly refused to pay his taxes. The authorities eventually sent troops to fetch and punish him. On the way to the capital, Mamas noticed a lion about to fall upon a lamb. He took up the lamb in his arms and rode into the capital on the lion's back. The Byzantine governor was so impressed that he released the hermit from his dues. Since then St.Mamas has been the patron saint of tax avoiders.

Description

The site of the present 18th century monastery church was originally occupied by a temple to Aphrodite. In the 15th century a church was erected which incorporated both Byzantine and Gothic features.

Elements of this structure, representing the flamboyant style of the late 15th century, were recycled as can be seen from the north portal, the capitals of the columns in the nave, and the arcade niches, which

ST.MAMAS - CAPITALS UNDER THE DOME (**Camille Enlart**)

81

display the consummate skills of the masons from the time of Helena Paleologinas. Ornamentation includes floral, and laurel, vine and fig foliage designs. The iconostasis is of particular interest: the marble panels of the lower part are richly carved with figs, grapes and acorns, and Venetian shields which once bore painted coats of arms; the upper part of carved wood painted blue and gold shows the mastery of the late 16th century woodcarvers.

An illustrated panel in the tympanum of the grave niche consists of many small icons representing scenes of martyrdom, painted in the local style. In the sarcophagus is a small opening through which a remedial balm is supposed to ooze, held to be effective against eye diseases and other illnesses. This *sweating stone* motif was very popular in Byzantine churches.

MUSEUM

The ground floor contains a natural science collection and upstairs archaeological finds are on display.

Archaeological Collection

Room I: Here can be seen the progressive development of pottery from the Early Stone Age when clay pots are not in evidence, through the Late Stone Age with *Red on White Ware*, and on to the *Red Polished Ware* of the Early Bronze Age. *White Painted Ware* and *Red on White* predominated during the Middle Bronze Age whilst *Base Ring* and *Red Lustrous Ware* was representative of the Late Bronze Age. The most remarkable object in this room is the terracotta figure of a bird-faced goddess. In the corridor, amphorae and jugs from the Geometric Period can be seen.

Rooms II & III display finds from the 'Toumba tou Skoura'.

Room IV: Notable in this room are the terracotta figures from the archaic period, including a model of a war chariot.

Room V contains pieces from Classical, Hellenistic and Roman times. The most significant item is a statue of Artemis wearing a cloak divided into squares by cords, and decorated with animal forms.

SURROUNDINGS OF GÜZELYURT

The district of Güzelyurt, which today is principally involved in the production of citrus fruit, became one of the most important cultural regions of Cyprus on account of the proximity of the copper mines, and its wind protected bay. Human settlement in the area stretches back to neolithic times and in the Bronze Age the first commercial town centres grew up, where copper was mined, processed and exported.

In the necropolis of Serhadköy, (Philia), archaeologists have found a type of red polished pottery similar to that discovered in western Anatolia, which suggests an influx of people from Anatolia who were perhaps fleeing from catastrophic events on the mainland. (c.2300 BC)

In Akdeniz, (Ayia Irini), a settlement and cultural continuity was established which lasted from the Iron Age up to Hellenistic times. The excavated ruins of the late Roman town of Soli can be traced back to classical times. Just three miles away on the hill top at Vouni, Swedish archaeologists laid bare the ruins of a palace complex dating from the 5th century BC, which showed both Greek and Persian influences.

These discoveries are evidence of the continuous economic and cultural evolution of this region.

Toumba tou Skourou

This site is located about two miles out of Güzelyurt on the way to Çamlıbel. Opposite a small hut and water pump on the right hand side, a narrow road leads off to the left. After about half a mile, a track branches off to the right to the site of the excavations where the slight remains of a temple and tombs are visible.

In the Early and Middle Bronze Age, Toumba tou Skourou was an important town centre where copper was worked and exported. As in Enkomi, the dead were buried in the yards of the houses; rich grave finds reflect the prosperity of this period. Red polished ware and white slip ware constitute the main mass of the pottery unearthed here. The occasional discovery of Minoan objects points to trading relations with Minoan Crete. The excavated objects are on display in the Güzelyurt Museum.

Güzelyurt

Ayia Irini

Continuing from Güzelyurt, on the outskirts of Tepebaşı (Dhiorios), a secondary road leads westwards to Akdeniz (Ayia Irini). The excavations are sitated near the church at the far end where Swedish archaeologists revealed the remains of a Temenos or sanctuary. In the centre of the site were found a fireplace, a table-like slab, tools of stone, olive stones and some large bowls. At the same time a huge collection of more than 2000 terracotta figures from the Archaic period - some of them life-size - was discovered. These are now displayed in the Cyprus Museum, in the Greek section of Nicosia. From 1970 to 1974 an Italian Expedition uncovered Hellenistic/Roman houses and part of a city wall; also several graves, some dating back to the Bronze Age.
Not accessible at present.

Çamlıbel(Myrtou)

The monastery of St. Panteleimon, the patron saint of physicians, is the principal monument of this village. The 18th century church was erected on the site of an earlier 16th century structure. Gunnis writes:
'The extremely interesting church has recently been restored, with the usual fatal results. The loggia, pointed arches, and vaulting have been torn down, and the floor of the church re-done with glazed and slippery tiles. The iconostasis is dated 1743. The chief icon is of St. Panteleimon .... dated 1770.' Not accessible at present.

A mile beyond Çamlıbel in the direction of Nicosia, a track branches to the right to the sanctuary of **Myrtou - Pigadhes**. In the middle of a Bronze Age Temenos stands an altar, which was restored after its discovery in 1952. The upper bull-shaped part refers to the Neolithic and Bronze Age culture of Çatal Hüyük in Anatolia. This ritual use of the bull is also depicted in the Temenos model found in the Necropolis of Vounous. (see page 49)

SOLI

From Güzelyurt, the road heads towards the southwest to Gemikonağı (Karavostasi), the 'mooring place for ships'. Here lies the harbour of ancient Soli. Even in this century copper ore from the mines of Skouriotissa and Mavrovouni (now in a military zone) was brought to Xeros, and then shipped from Gemikonağı. The conveyer belts of the Cyprus Mines Corporation still jut out into the sea.
The turnoff to Soli is signposted.

84

There is some evidence that a town existed on the site of Soli as far back as 700 BC, when it is referred to as Sillu in an Assyrian tribute list. In 580 BC, King Philokypros is said to have removed his capital from Aepia to Sillu on the advice of Solon, the Athenian philosopher, and to have renamed it Soli in honour of his mentor.

Whatever its origin, the town was well placed,with a good water supply, close to fertile plains and with a protected harbour at its disposal. The copper mines nearby guaranteed its wealth.

In 498 BC, Soli along with the other city kingdoms of Cyprus, Amathus excepted, rose against their Persian masters. The Ionians sent a fleet to aid the uprising, and defeated the Phoenicians, allies of the Persians, at sea. However, on land, the Cypriots were routed by the Persian forces, with Aristokypros, the king of Soli, falling in battle. The Persians then besieged Soli, which fell after five months.

In Roman times Soli was a flourishing city, but by the 4th century AD, its importance waned as its harbour silted up and the copper mines were closed. Saracen pirates destroyed the town in the 7th century AD.

The Basilica of Soli

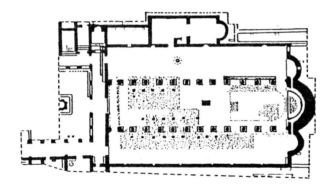

BASILICA OF SOLI: GROUND PLAN

This early Christian basilica was built on a man made terrace about 200 yards east of the acropolis. Roman coins found on the site indicate that the church was first built in the latter half of the 4th century. The floor of this three aisled building was laid with mosaics in figurative and ornamental design. Parts still remains, including some duck and fish

motifs in the north east section. To the west of the three entrance portals, a narthex opened on to an atrium (only partially excavated). In the middle is the marble base of the fountain which once occupied this position. To the east, in the principal apse, an inscription pleads:
"O Christ, save those who gave this mosaic".

During the 5th and 6th centuries the basilica was enlarged, and additions were made, but during the saracens raids of the 7th century, the building was razed.

In the 12th century a new, but much smaller church was built on the ruins, the remains of which can be seen in the eastern part of the basilica.

Roman Theatre

Further up the hill lies the 2nd century theatre which was excavated by the Swedish Cyprus Expedition in 1929 and later restored by the Department of Antiquities. The auditorium has a diameter of 170ft and a capacity of about 3500 people. The raised stage once had two stories, and was richly adorned with marble panelling and statues: only a few column fragments hint at its former opulence. This *Hellenistic Type* of theatre, which exploits the contours of the hillside in its construction, is similar to those of Aspendos and Temessos.

A couple of hundred yard west of the theatre, archaeologists stumbled upon an extensive temple complex where, besides various terracotta and marble pieces, the *Aphrodite of Soli* was found. The clue to this discovery came from a passage by the geographer Strabo, and other ancient texts.

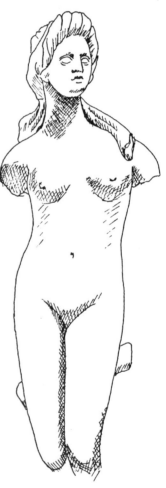

APHRODITE OF SOLI

THEATRE OF SOLI
(AFTER EXCAVATION BY THE SWEDISH CYPRUS EXPEDITION)

PALACE OF VOUNI

A few miles west of Soli is the palace of Vouni, prominently placed on a hilltop rising sheer from the sea.

After the failed uprising against the Persians in 498 BC, the pro-Persian king of Marion, possibly a Phoenician, built the palace as a stronghold and vantage point to watch over the pro-Greek city of Soli.

The principal structure has been shown to be of the oriental Liwan type. In 449 BC, after his victory over the Persians in Cyprus, the Athenian general Cimon replaced the king of Marion with a pro-Greek prince. This political change was accompanied by architectural alterations resulting in a megaron type structure typical of the palaces in Mycenaean Greece. The palace was destroyed by fire in 380 BC.

Description

The hilltop at Vouni was excavated in the late 1920's by the Swedish Cyprus Expedition, and has been described in a very readable account by Gjerstad himself. (see bibliography) A basic description is offered here.

87

The palace can be divided broadly into two building phases, representing the pro-Persian, and then the pro-Greek rulers. The core of the original palace consisted of a tripartite system of state apartments (1), (2), and (3), entered from the south west, (E1). The middle section is divided into three, with an entrance hall leading into the main room, and an inner hall beyond. The flanking sections form a series of interconnecting rooms. A broad flight of seven steps leads down from the state apartments to a peristyle courtyard (4) enclosed on its remaining three sides by rooms which open on to the courtyard. The arrangement described so far is the Cypriot expression of oriental *Liwan* architecture.

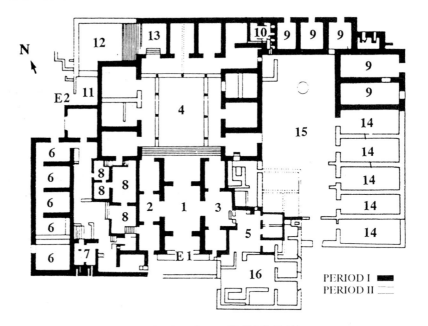

PALACE OF VOUNI - GROUND PLAN

Additional structures include kitchen buildings (5) to the south east, and to the north west, a complex of store-rooms (6), bathrooms (7), and living quarters (8). Some of the store-rooms have holes in the ground for receiving the pointed ends of amphorae, in which wine and oil were stored. In the eastern corner are more store-rooms (9), accessed from outside, and also a hot bath (10), or sudatorium, one of the earliest examples on record.

When the Greek rulers took over the palace in c.449 BC, they walled off the entrance (E1), thus transforming section (1) into a *Megaron* type structure. The entrance was relocated to the northern corner (E2). A ramp (11) led up to an angled vestibule (12) from where a flight of steps gave access to an ante-room, (13). This ante-room opened on to the central courtyard. More store-rooms (14) were built to the east, enclosing a courtyard (15). There were also extensive additions and modifications to the kitchen arrangements in the south east, (16). A second storey was also added to the palace, with walls made from mud bricks.

Water supplies for the palace were stored in underground cisterns, carved out of the rock under the courtyards. These were filled from the winter rains. In the central courtyard stands a stone stele, one of a pair which supported a windlass used for drawing water from the cistern.

During excavations, the *Treasure of Vouni* was found in a clay pot, blackened by the fire which destroyed the palace. Exquisitely finished bracelets of gold and silver, finely worked silver bowls, along with hundreds of coins, were brought to the light of day 2300 years after their concealment. Most of the coins were from the city of Marion, with some from Lapithos, Kition and Paphos. One came from Amathus.

To the south are the remains of a temple to Athena, where a mass of votive offerings were discovered, and where three fine bronze sculptures were uncovered. One depicts a cow, and the other two show two lions falling upon a bull.

Lefke

In Gemikonağı (Karavostasi), a road branches off to the south to the old Turkish village of Lefke, lying amidst orange groves and date palms. Here and there amongst the old Turkish houses, it can be seen how the Ottoman architects adopted certain elements of Gothic and classical forms. In the middle ages, Lefke was one of the chief baronies in the Cyprus, and was the origin in 1426 of an island wide uprising of the peasants.

Koruçam (Kormakiti)

Southeast of Çamlıbel (Myrtou), a road leads off in a north westerly direction to Kormakiti, the biggest Maronite village in Cyprus. The Maronites originate from adherents to a Syrian Christian church in the Lebanon. They first settled in Cyprus in the 9th century.

Güzelyurt

In the centre of Koruçam is the large church of St. George, which, according to Gunnis, *'is a good example of modern building and in excellent taste'*. When it was finished, the Maronites handed over their former church, also dedicated to St.George, to the Franciscan order. The 15th century church of St.George is a single aisled building with buttressed walls and barrel vaulting. Corbels supporting the transverse arches are in places ornamented with crosses. An inscription in Aramaic on the wooden doors of the south portal blesses those who cross that threshold. The convent is still occupied by Franciscan nuns who minister to the Maronite families remaining in the village.

FAMAGUSTA / GAZİMAĞUSA

I have seen old ships sail like swans asleep
Beyond the village which men still call Tyre,
With leaden age o'ercargoed, dipping deep
For Famagusta and the hidden sun
That rings black Cyprus with a lake of fire;
And all those ships were certainly so old...

J.E.Flecker

History

After the final destruction of Salamis/Constantia in 648, the inhabitants settled in the small lagoon town of Arsinoe, founded in 260 BC by Ptolemaios, a successor of Alexander the Great. In allusion to the fate of Salamis, the settlers called their town *Ammochostos* (hidden in sand), which later became corrupted to Famagusta.

The population increased when the Byzantine emperor John Comnenos allowed Armenian refugees to settle, who had been ousted from their territory by the Seljuks.

However, it was the crusades that stimulated the growth of Famagusta into a major city, a halfway house for businessmen and pilgrims alike as they journeyed to and from the holy land. The fall of Acre in 1291 resulted in a mass exodus of the Christians in Syria and Palestine, and the gates of Famagusta were opened to them by the Lusignan king of Cyprus, Henry II.

This influx of people, along with their skills, caused Famagusta to develop rapidly into one of the wealthiest cities in the known world, the principal emporium connecting east and west. Many european trading houses established themselves here, as did military and religious orders. The Italian coastal republics also founded colonies, and it was as a result of a dispute between the Genoese and the Venetians that Famagusta fell into Genoese hands.

The argument centred on who would lead the king's horse during the coronation of Peter II in 1373. Events led to a massacre of the Genoese, who thereupon despatched an armada which seized the city and held it until it was recaptured by James II in 1464.

91

The partial abandonment of the town after the Genoese conquest led to a rapid decline in the prosperity of Famagusta in the latter decades of the 14th century, as witnessed by Nicholas Martoni who wrote of his visit in 1394:

'The city of Famagusta is as large, I reckon, as the city of Capua, and has fine squares, and houses very much like those of Capua, but a great part, almost a third, is unihabited, and the houses are destroyed, and this has been done since the date of the Genoese lordship.'

By the time the Venetians took over Cyprus in 1489, the city was half empty.

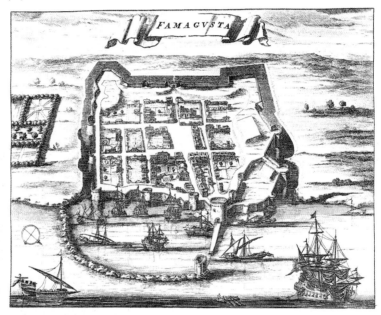

The Lusignan defences of Cyprus were rendered obsolete by the invention of gunpowder, and the Venetians undertook a major rebuilding program in Famagusta, Kyrenia and Nicosia. Their efforts were in vain, for barely had they finished the defences than Ottoman forces invaded the island, and Famagusta eventually surrendered after a long and desperate struggle in 1571.

Over the next 300 years, the city went to rack and ruin, and a traveller in the mid 18th century estimated the population to be no more than 300.

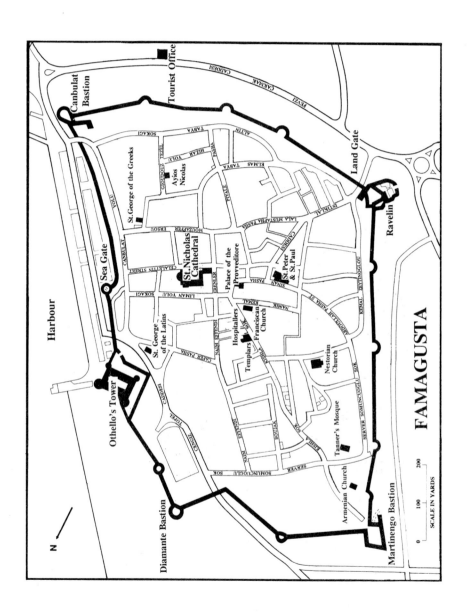

THE WALLED CITY OF FAMAGUSTA

Description

Famagusta is surrounded by massive Venetian walls, up to 50 ft. high and 25 ft. thick, and fortified at intervals by bastions. Giovanni Sanmichele, who designed the defences, did not live to see his ideas realized, succumbing to fever in 1559. There were originally two entrances - a land gate protected by the ravelin, and a sea gate about 200 yards to the south-east of the citadel. These gates were once linked, via the main square, by the partially covered bazaar street. The palaces and mansions of diplomats and the rich, which once lined Kishla street, have now vanished and only the city walls and a few churches survive to tell the tale.

Protecting the *landgate* was the great *ravelin,* a defensive structure projecting from the walls, which was the scene of some of the fiercest fighting during the siege of 1571. It was captured and occupied by the assailants at one stage, but was immediately blown up by the defenders, with massive loss of life. It was later rebuilt by the invaders.

From the town side this bastion can be entered through the huge 30ft. archway: inside are various chambers and dungeons. To the right of the arch is the ramp up which the cannons were drawn, to the gunnery platform above.

At the north-western corner of the city is the massive master-piece of Venetian engineering, the *Martinengo Bastion.* The Ottoman besiegers regarded it as impregnable, and did not attempt to assault it. In 1966 two colossal underground vaults were discovered, the purpose of which is not entirely clear.

Othello's Tower

The *citadel,* in the north east, was built by the Lusignans in the 14th century to protect the harbour, and followed the plan of the crusader castles along the coast of Palestine. It was originally surrounded by a moat.In 1492 the citadel was rebuilt by the Venetians as an artillery stronghold. Stone faced earthworks were thrown up around the old square towered Lusignan fortress, similar to the changes wrought on Kyrenia castle. The upper floor was dismantled and round towers were added with cannon emplacements, from which the fosse alongside the walls could be enfiladed. On a marble panel above the main entrance is carved the winged lion of Venice, and the name of Nicolo Foscarini, who remodelled the citadel.

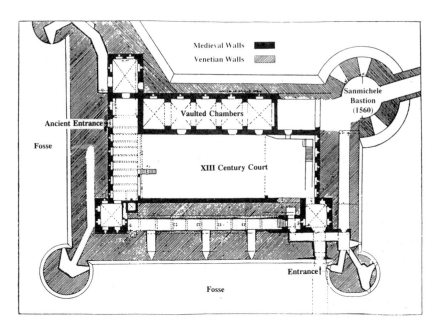

PLAN OF THE CITADEL

The entrance leads into a square Frankish tower to the left of which is a long corridor leading to several cannon emplacements; to the right, a dark passage (bring a torch) leads down to further artillery chambers in the adjacent round tower. Note the ventilation shafts. Beyond the entrance lies a spacious inner court, facing which is the well preserved vaulted refectory from the 14th century. To the right of the refectory, a doorway opens into a chamber, the site of the Frankish NE tower, from which the present round NE tower may be accessed. Upstairs, above the refectory, remains of the former apartments are apparent, including several window seats. A model showing the various building phases can be seen in the ticket office.

The alternative name *"Othello's Tower"* came into use during the British colonial period. Shakespeare's tragedy was set in a seaport in Cyprus, and Othello, the Moor of Venice, has been identified with a Venetian governor of Cyprus, Christophoro Moro, whose surname means 'moor'. It is known that he returned to Venice without his wife, but it is left to playwrights to speculate as to the reason why. (For a detailed discussion of this topic, see chapter 8 in Sir Harry Luke's *Cyprus*.)

The elegant *sea gate*, south east of Othello's Tower, is evidence that Venetian military architecture is not always purely utilitarian. The name of Nicolo Prioli, who built it in 1496, is inscribed above the gate, on the seaward side, along with the lion of St.Mark. The original iron portcullis is still in place. To one side of the gate, on the inside, is a large marble lion. It is supposed to open its mouth once a year, yielding treasure to the person brave enough to pluck it from its throat.

ST.NICHOLAS CATHEDRAL (Lala Mustapha Pasha Mosque)

History

The earliest document relating to the cathedral dates from the year 1300, when a certain Isabel of Antioch bequeathed a considerable sum of money for its construction, on the understanding that she should be buried within its precincts. Work began under the Latin bishop of Famagusta, Guy d'Ibelin, and continued in 1308 under Bishop Baldwin Lambert. An inscription placed by the latter on the south aisle portal is dated 1311, and specifies the number of vaults already in place. The consecration ceremony took place in 1326. Up until 1372, when the Genoese took over Famagusta, St.Nicholas was the venue for the kings of Cyprus to add the token crown of Jerusalem to their collection.

James II married Caterina Cornaro in the cathedral in 1472, and it was here, 17 years later, that Caterina signed her abdication in favour of the Doge of Venice, thus ending the Lusignan Dynasty. After the Ottoman conquest, the cathedral was converted into a mosque, called initially Aysofya Cami, and later changed to Lala Mustapha Pasha Mosque, after the Ottoman general who conquered Cyprus.

Description

St.Nicholas cathedral is one of the most impressive pieces of Gothic architecture in Cyprus. It does not have as much small scale decoration as St.Sophia in Nicosia, but it more elegantly proportioned, and its shallow porches permit a better view of the fine tracery window above the nave entrance. The limited decoration on the door arches perhaps emphasises the fine carving of the statue canopies and brackets on either side of the central doorway. The statues have long since vanished, but their tiny vaulted canopies decorated with finials and crockets have survived and are masterpieces in miniature.

The western façade overlooking the main square is the best preserved and most impressive part of the building. The cathedral was severely damaged during the siege of 1571, losing most of its flying buttresses, but it was patched up afterwards, and converted into a mosque, a minaret being added to the north tower.

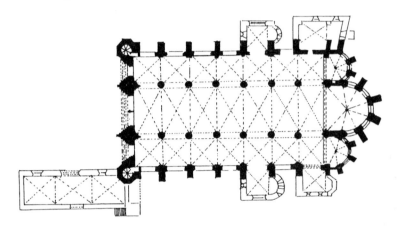

ST. NICHOLAS CATHEDRAL - GROUND PLAN

The inside consists of a nave and two aisles with side chapels and a triple apsed choir. Two rows of massive round columns support the ceiling vaulting; as in St.Sophia, there is no triforium, and the cathedral is not as lofty as its European counterparts. (Cyprus is subject to earthquakes, lying as it does between the European and African tectonic plates. The architecture consequently tends to be squat and solid.) The upper windows in the western part of the building are well preserved and worthy of note, as are the rosette and lancet windows in the apse.

The grave plaques which were built into the floor have mostly disappeared, and none remain to commemorate the kings of Cyprus and Jerusalem.

In the north of the forecourt is a domed building which used to be a Koran school, and opposite is a 16th century Venetian building now used for Islamic ablutions. The decorated doorway is flanked by two round windows above which Venetian coats of arms can still be seen. In front of the building is a 20 ft. long marble frieze, a spoil from Salamis, depicting frolicking animals.

Palazzo del Proveditore

Opposite the cathedral are the remains of the royal palace of the Lusignanas. The facade is a Venetian addition, and the arms of Giovanni Renier, Captain of Cyprus in 1552, can be seen over the central arch. During the Ottoman era, the palace was used as a prison, its most notable captive being Mehmed Namık Kemal (1840 - 1888), the most celebrated Ottoman poet, who was exiled for defying the sultan.

Church of St.Francis

Next to the palace lie the ruins of the church of St.Francis, once part of an extensive monastery founded by Henry II, a great supporter of the Franciscan order, in about 1300. His successor, Hugh IV, who favoured the Dominican order, turned the passage connecting the church to the royal palace into a rifle range.

The church consists of a nave with two side chapels, and a polygonal choir. The multiprofiled cross ribbed vaulting rests upon corbels decorated with foliage designs.

Nestorian Church

This church, built in the 14th century by a wealthy merchant, originally comprised a nave and choir, the aisles and bell tower being later additions. The vaulting, which is not ribbed, is supported on figuratively carved corbels. Note the darker toned stone used for the keystones. The side windows are simple, bevelled lancet windows without tracery. The entrance portal is plain, with a circular window above.

Mural fragments can still be seen in the apse, along with some inscriptions in Syrian, the liturgic language of the Nestorians.

The Church of St.Peter and St.Paul

This bulky and rather graceless church is another mid 14th century product. It is well preserved, and its sturdy construction has saved it from the fate suffered by the Orthodox cathedral.(St. George of the Greeks) As in St.Nicholas cathedral, the cross ribbed vaulting is supported on round columns with flat capitals. Decoration inside is limited to the vaulting bosses, which are carved with a rosette of leaves. The main entrance portal to the north aisle reveals a quality of workmanship equal to that of St.George of the Latins, and may have been imported from another church.

The nave vaulting is supported by plain flying buttresses; an extra row was added to support the south aisle wall after earthquakes in the 16th century. In the south west corner is a small spiral staircase, used by the Moslems to ascend the minaret which was added when the church was converted into a mosque.

St.George of the Greeks

This unique 15th century ruin was once the orthodox cathedral of Famagusta. It is unusual in that it combines both Gothic and Byzantine architectural elements in its structure.

The ground plan follows that of St.Peter and St.Paul, but the Byzantine style apse is much higher, reaching the level of the Gothic vaulting in the nave. The church was statically vulnerable on account of inadequate buttressing, but natural collapse was pre-empted by the Ottoman bombardment in 1571. In the middle apse, rows of steps can be seen, and this feature, borrowed from early Christian basilicas, indicates that St.George was the church of a bishop.

Adjacent to the cathedral are the ruins of a Byzantine church comprising two aisles and two apses, which was once the resting place of the renowned archbishop of Salamis, St.Epiphanios of Constantia. (310-406)

St.George of the Latins

The ruins which lie about 200 yards south of Othello's Tower may pre-date the city walls, as there is evidence that St.George of the Latins was a fortified church: traces of a crenellated parapet remain, in addition to the watch tower on the north west corner. This would suggest that it was constructed at the end of the 13th century, probably from materials taken from a Roman temple in Salamis.

Of particular interest is the way in which the slender Gothic attached columns have been carved from the classic pillars, the round sandstone drums of which are displaced to the left and right on alternate rows, thus keying into the wall. These drums are all 33cm thick, so that three courses of masonry with the mortar joints measures exactly one metre. The carved capitals are much eroded, but deeply cut foliar motifs may be discerned, and also an unusual design depicting winged dragons. A niche above the altar no doubt displayed an image of St. George.

Only the north door has survived, but it is clear that a corresponding door to the south existed, in addition to the western entrance. The sacristy, entered through the north east angle of the apse, retains its vaulting.

Though the western façade, the south wall and the roof are absent, the tall, elegant stature of this church is still evident from the remaining north wall and choir. Large and lofty windows, once embellished with tracery, graced the sides and choir, and the ribbed vaulting sprayed up to keystones which now lie fallen on the floor of the nave.

The Twin Churches

The crusader knights of the Temple and Hospital orders once owned these churches. The larger of the two was built by the Templars at the beginning of the 14th century, and dedicated to St.Anthony. Three doorways in the north wall of this single aisled building once opened on to an adjoining cloister. The church was taken over by the Hospitallers upon the dissolution of the Temple order by the Pope in 1313. The adjacent tower-like chapel of the Hospitallers preserves its flagstaff sockets high up on the west wall: this unusual feature was also adopted by Orthodox and Maronite churches in the Levant. In the vicinity of the twin churches, architectural details from Frankish and Venetian times can be seen, incorporated into Ottoman and Turkish buildings.

SURROUNDINGS OF FAMAGUSTA

The district surrounding Famagusta is one is one of the most interesting in the Mediterranean basin, for here are concentrated the archaeological remains of several important eras: the Bronze Age town of Enkomi, the Iron Age royal tombs, ancient Salamis, the Byzantine monastery of St.Barnabas, and Famagusta during the middle ages.

Settlement in the area goes back to Neolithic times. Settlers from Asia Minor and the Syrian/Palestine region landed here and left behind their archaeological traces. Towards the end of the Middle Bronze Age, highly organised communities were established, such as Enkomi, where copper was worked and exported. In the 14th and 15th centuries BC, Enkomi, along with Ugarit, its neighbour on the Syrian coast, was the most important trading centre in the Near East. Rich finds of Minoan and Mycenaean pottery point to trading relations with Minoan Crete and Mycenaean centres in the Peloponnese.

The Achaeans from Mycenae had already begun to settle in Enkomi by the 13th century BC, so when the Doric migrations displaced them from their homeland, in the 11th century, Cyprus was a logical target for colonisation. There is some evidence that Enkomi was destroyed by earthquakes during the 11th century, and that its river harbour had silted up. This may explain why the Achaean colonists established a new capital at Salamis, nearer to the sea.

Little is known of the next two centuries but it is clear that when Cyprus re-emerged, it had been transformed into a Greek island in language, culture and religion.

In the following centuries Salamis played a leading role amongst the city kingdoms in the island, and took part in the uprising of the Ionian coastal towns against the Persians. During Hellenistic and Roman times, Salamis remained a major economic and political centre in the eastern Mediterranean.

The city was rebuilt in the 4th century AD after earthquake damage, and renamed Constantia, in honour of the Roman Emperor Constantius. Further earthquakes, the silting of its harbour, and raids by Arab pirates led to the eventual abandonment of the town. The inhabitants settled in the neighbouring harbour town of Arsinoe, which later became Famagusta.

When, with the fall of Acre in 1291, the Christians lost their toehold in Palestine, Famagusta, next to Alexandria, became the most important trading centre linking east and west.

SALAMIS

The first excavations at Salamis were carried out by stone and grave robbers, followed by amateur archaeologists in the 19th century, who enriched the British Museum with their finds.

Systematic excavations began in the 1950s and 60s under the direction of J.Pouilloux and V.Karageorghis, who laid bare an archaic

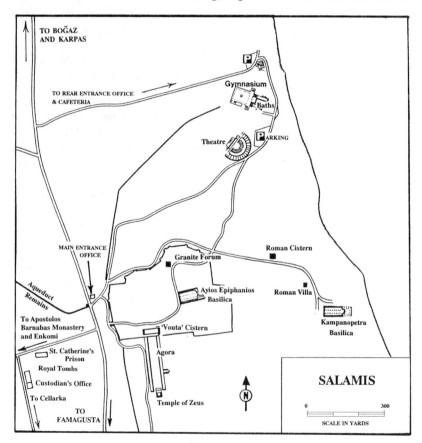

necropolis. Operations ceased in 1974, and most of the city remains under the sand, below a forest of acacias.

The Achaean colonisation of the island is reflected in the local mythology: Teucer, one of the Achaean heroes of the Iliad, was banished by his father, Telamon, king of the Greek island of Salamis. Teucer landed on the north coast of Cyprus, on the *Achaeans Beach*, and then founded a city at the mouth of the Pedios river which he named after his homeland. Even in Roman times, noble families traced their lineage back to Teucer, and regarded him as the founder of Salamis and the Temple of Zeus.

Archaeological traces show the existence of a town, with a harbour and necropolis dating from the 11th century BC. In the 8th century BC, after the intervening 'Dark Ages', Salamis expanded greatly to become an important trading centre. The necropolis, or *Royal Tombs*, discovered near the town, yielded contents which shed light on the rites and customs of that time.

6th century texts and coins bring Salamis into the historical era. The first Cypriot coins were minted in Salamis during the reign of Evelthon.

In the early 5th century BC, the flames of revolt against their Persian masters by the Ionian states spread to Cyprus. However, King Gorgos of Salamis, a descendant of Evelthon, would not lend his support to the struggle. Thereupon Onesilos, backed by the majority of the island's cities, deposed his brother, who fled to the Persians. The Persians then crossed over to Cyprus, protected by a Phoenician fleet, and annihilated the cypriot forces on the plains before Salamis, Onesilos being amongst those slain.

In 411 BC, Evagoras, a descendent of the Teucer dynasty, seized the throne of Salamis from the pro-persian usurper Abdemon. Evagoras fostered trade, reformed the defences of the city, and pursued his goal of casting off the Persian yoke. In this he failed, as did his successors until the time of Alexander.

Alexander the Great smashed the Persian Empire (334 BC), and after his death, Cyprus came under his successors in Egypt, the Ptolemies.

During the Hellenistic and Roman period, Salamis experienced a resurgence of cultural and commercial activity, interrupted by earthquakes in the years 76, 77, 332, and 342 AD.

103

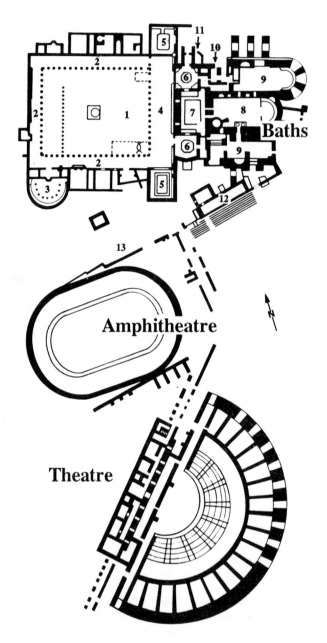

PLAN OF THE MAIN EXCAVATED SITES **(After Karageorghis)**

In 45 AD, St.Barnabus, a native of Salamis, came to proselytize in Cyprus, and during a subsequent visit, in 52 AD, was martyred in his home town.

The large community of Jews in Salamis, unhappy about the eclipse of their religion by the Christians, revolted in 115, massacring thousands of Greeks. Emperor Trajan sent Roman troops to crush the rebellion, and all Jews were subsequently banished from the island.

In the mid 4th century, Constantius II rebuilt Salamis, which had been destroyed by an earthquake, and renamed it *Constantia*. After further natural catastrophes, raids of Arab pirates,and the silting up of its harbour, the city was abandoned, the remaining inhabitants removing to Arsinoe, a few miles to the south.

The Baths and Gymnasium

This complex, along with the theatre, forum, and amphitheatre, constituted the hub of public life in the city.

The site consists of a peristyle court (1), used as an exercise ground for the athletes, and a series of adjoining baths. There used to be a stone basin in the middle of the court in the time of Augustus, but this was replaced by a podium with a column surmounted with a statue of an emperor.

During the restorations of the 4th century, the broken columns of the Stoa (2) were replaced by marble columns with corinthian capitals taken from the ruins of the nearby amphitheatre. This recycling of building materials explains the diverse forms of the columns,capitals, and bases.

In the southwest corner are the latrines, with seating for 44 people. (3) The flushing system is worth examining: a water conduit pierces the arc in the middle, feeding a basin which can exit below, for flushing, or can overflow into an open channel running along the rim of the arc. This channel supplied clean water with which users could clean themselves. A small set of latrines (11) may be seen to the north of the baths. Its mosaic floor is still intact.

The eastern Stoa (4), richly furnished with opus sectile, serves as the entrance to the baths. It is flanked by two annexes (5) containing swimming pools. The northern annexe has many sculptures following classical themes. The baths comprise two octagonal frigidaria (6), between which is the central sudatorium, or sweating room (7), where part of the hypocaust (floor heating) remains. Hot air circulated between the brick columns, heating the floor. On the south wall is a mural dating from the 3rd century AD depicting Hylas refusing the water nymphs. The calderium (8), or hot water bath (note hypocaust in the apse), adjoins the central sudatorium, and is flanked by two additional sudatoria (9). In the southern sudatorium, accessed from outside, there are two mosaics: Apollo and Artemis kill Niobes children with arrows; Leda and the swan with the river god Eurotas. Two further mosaics may be seen in the north walls of the calderium and the northern sudatorium. The Praefurnium, or furnace room, lies to the north of the baths. (10)

The tunnel-like structure (12) just south of the baths was probably a water cistern, fed by an aqueduct (13), leading from the west. This cistern was plastered internally: traces remain in the corners. Two exit conduits are visible in the wall in the section where the roof is intact.

Theatre

This theatre dates from the time of Augustus. The semicircular orchestra is 84 ft in diameter and was originally paved with marble tiles of varying hue. At the focal point was an altar dedicated to the god Dionysus. The auditorium, consisting of some 50 rows of seats (not all have been restored), had a capacity of at least 15,000, and is divided into sectors by eight flights of steps. The original limestone dressing is still extant on the lower tiers of seats and higher up, in the middle sector, the seats of honour can be seen where the VIPs would sit. The inner half of the auditorium rested on a solid foundation, but the upper tiers were supported by radial walls linked by arches.

In contrast to Greek theatre, action in the Roman theatre took place not in the orchestra, but on a raised proscenium, or stage, and remains of its 130 ft. foundation wall can still be seen. Columns were placed in the foreground, and the proscenium was decorated with statues.

The earthquakes of the 4th century AD caused the collapse of this massive structure; it was never rebuilt and soon became a source of building materials. Excavations brought to light statues of Apollo and the muses, carved in the style of the Ionian coastal towns.

FURTHER REMAINS

To view the rest of the remains, turn back along the road from the theatre, keeping to the left at the fork just beyond the gateposts.

Turning left at the crossroads about a quarter of a mile further on, the road leads down towards the sea. A Roman villa may be discerned on the right hand side, up a short track, identifiable by a galvanised corrugated roof over part of the ruins; before the villa, and on the other side of the road, is a Roman cistern. This cistern contains some extraordinary murals including one of the earliest representations of Christ on the island. It may have been a secret meeting place for the early Christians. *Equipment is necessary for safe access.* Continuing on the road down to the sea, the ruins of a large basilica may be seen on the left hand side. Returning to the crossroads and turning left, the road passes the granite forum (rhs), the water clock, and the basilica of Ayios Epiphanios (lhs). Following the road around to the left, the road passes by a huge Byzantine cistern, the agora, and the temple of Zeus on the left hand side.

Roman Villa

Overlooking the sea, this Roman villa consists of an apsidial reception hall and a central inner court with a columned portico. The sleeping and living quarters are grouped about the inner court. A well supplying water for the villa is located in the wall near the south west corner of the courtyard. The house was also equipped with a conduit system, which was integrated into the floor. After the abandonment of the city, the villa was used as a goods yard and as an oil mill.(Note the large stone crushing bowl in the apse of the reception room, along with mill stones, and a curious straining device on the right hand side.) The first two steps of a spiral staircase may be observed on the far side, suggesting that an upper storey once existed. Graffiti indicates that the mill was still in use in the Middle Ages.

Kampanopetra Basilica

This basilica, which is situated not far from the ancient harbour, is an architectural document of the significance of Christianity, the state religion, in late Roman times. The 4th century building comprises three aisles, and two narrow outer gangways, to which the baptismal candidates retired after the catechism, before the mass was conducted. Several marble coffins may be seen in the gangway on the south side.

In the main apse, part of the synthronon remains, where the bishop's throne, and the seats of the presbyters were located. The church porch to the west adjoins a peristyle atrium, in the middle of which was a well for ablution, a typical feature of eastern basilicas. To the east of the church is another atrium, beyond which is a group of buildings which appear to have housed bathing facilities, and a sudatorium. Within this complex lies a mosaic floor of exceptional beauty, not to be overlooked.

Ayios Epiphanios Basilica

Measuring 190 by 135 ft, the largest known basilica in Cyprus was built as the metropolitan church of Salamis/Constantia during the office of Bishop Epiphanios. (368-403)

Archaeologists have laid bare the nave, separated from aisles on each side by two rows of 14 stone columns with corinthian capitals. Each aisle is associated with two gangways for the catechumens. The broad nave terminates in a semi-circular apse, equipped with a stepped synthronon. On each side of the apse are chambers which served a dressing room for the priests, and for storage of liturgical apparatus. Hypocaust remains in the baptistry to the south-east of the basilica show that initiates were spared a cold immersion in its eastern processionary style font.

The bishop's tomb lies cased in marble before the southern apse. His remains were apparently removed and re-interred in Constantinople by the Byzantine Emperor Leon. (886-912) Immediately behind the tomb, a small church was erected after the destruction of the basilica in the 7th century. This church, with a nave and two aisles, was rebuilt in the 9th century, when the roof over the nave was replaced by three domes.

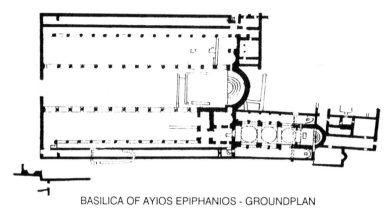

BASILICA OF AYIOS EPIPHANIOS - GROUNDPLAN

Water Reservoir 'Vouta'

Just before the Agora is the large water reservoir of the late Roman town of Salamis/Constantia. Inside the massive walls are the remnants of three rows of square pillars and twelve pairs of massive corbels projecting from the walls on either side, which once carried the vaulting. An exit conduit for the water can be seen at floor level in the excavated section, on the far side. The cistern was referred to by Martoni in 1394:

...a certain ancient cistern, no bigger one I think is found in the world, with a vault raised on thirty-six columns and with apertures above whence the water was drawn. Into this tank water flowed continuously from a certain mountain, along a conduit built with pillars and arches....

A 35 mile long aqueduct carried water to the town from its source in Değirmenlik (Kythrea), and remained in operation into the 7th century. The town had a system of pipes and conduits which fed the various cisterns and water tanks. The pipes were made up from short lengths of pottery tube formed on a wheel, with male and female ends, and joined together with a lime cement mixture.

Opposite the entrance ticket office on the other side of the main road, a dirt road may be found bearing off to the north west. This road follows the route of the aqueduct, and several complete arches may be seen about a mile down the track.

Agora or Stone Forum

According to an inscription, the agora, which was the market and meeting place of the town, was restored during the time of Augustus. It is likely that its history goes back to Hellenistic times. Surrounded by columned galleries, the agora was furnished with statues, altars, and benches, and adjacent to the long sides were public buildings and shops, some of them dressed with marble.

With one exception, only stubs of the columns remain on either side of this gigantic market place.

Temple of Zeus

Just south of the agora, the temple dedicated to Zeus was one of the principal temples of Salamis whose right to grant asylum was confirmed by Augustus in 22 AD. Inscriptions in honour of Livia, Augustus' consort, and of the olympian Zeus were discovered in 1890. Excavations have revealed traces of an earlier Hellenistic temple beneath the present ruins.

ROYAL TOMBS

The tumuli of the so called Royal Tombs, especially the barrel roof of St. Catherine's Prison, are clearly visible from afar. On the road from Salamis to the monastery of St. Barnabas, the first turning to the left leads to the tombs, and a small museum next to the custodians office.

Excavations brought to light an elaborate tomb architecture, and significant finds which not only shed light on the living standard and material culture of the time, but also demonstrated the survival of Mycenaean burial customs, as portrayed in Homer's Iliad. Most of the tombs had already been plundered, and the most significant discoveries of the archaeologists were made in the dromoi, the trapezoidal entrances of the burial chambers.

In the context of Mycenaean tomb architecture, the discovered remains of food for the departed, and human and equine sacrifices forces the attention to the 23rd song of the Iliad, describing the burial of the hero Patroclus. Since this interment has its counterpart in reality, may not other parts of the Homeric myths also be founded upon actual events?

In general, the grave sites consist of a trapezoidal dromos (where the bloody sacrifices took place) leading down to the propylaeum, or entrance porch, in front of the burial chamber. Large well hewn limestone blocks were used in the construction.

Tomb 47

During excavations in 1964, archaeologists stumbled upon several skeletons of horses in the dromos of this tomb. Two of the skeletons, which belong to an initial interment dating from the 8th century BC, were left in situ, to help the visitor to visualise the macabre rites of the past. A horsedrawn hearse brought the corpse into the dromos from the town, and after the body was placed in the burial chamber, the horses were slain as a mark of respect to the dead man.

In the 7th century BC, the tomb was prepared for a second interment. In a layer about 3 ft. above the present floor level, excavators found the remains of six horses, along with harnesses and blinkers made of bronze and ivory.

Tomb 79

Stratigraphic evidence shows that two interments took place in this tomb: the first at the end of the 8th century BC, and the second at the beginning of the 7th century BC.

The vast quantity of opulent finds in the dromos attests the power and wealth of the ancient kings of Salamis. Several chariots were found, along with horses with their harnesses and other accessories, including bronze breastplates covered with animal and human figures from Assyrian mythology. Side pendant ornaments show the Phoenician goddess Ishtar standing naked on the backs of two lions, holding lions in her hands. A wooden throne inlaid with ivory was also found, in addition to many carved ivory plaques, some of them gilt. On one of the plaques a representation of the god Heh is repeated six times to form a decorative frieze. A beautifully depicted winged sphynx wearing the crowns of Upper and Lower Egypt is the subject of an open-work carving, also in ivory. Large amphorae and quantities of other pottery were found in the dromos, including dishes still containing chicken and fish bones.

Tomb 50

Known as St.Catherine's Prison, this tomb was frequently used and rebuilt from the 8th century BC up until Roman times. In the 4th century AD the propylaeum was converted into a vaulted room. Scholars and travellers of the Middle Ages refer to the structure as the prison of St.Catherine, who was held captive in the time of Emperor Maxentius. According to legend, this Cypriot princess was converted by Jesus in a dream. Maxentius had her flogged and thrown into prison. The wheel on which she was whipped was destroyed by thunderbolts, but the unrelenting emperor had her head lopped off with a sword. Angels carried her corpse off to Mt.Sinai.

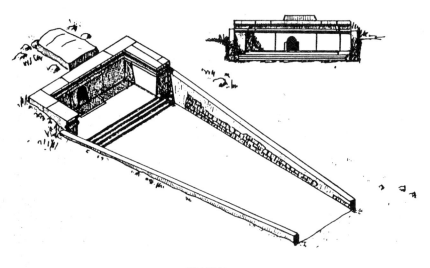

TOMB No. 50

The Homeric Tombs

In *tomb 1*, excavators discovered large quantities of Greek pottery, with motif designs from Attica, Euboea and Crete. Lined along the walls of the dromos were large amphorae, which may have contained oil and wine, as described in the Iliad.

In *tomb 3*, one amphora bore the painted label *of olive oil*, written in Cypriot syllabary. Two war chariots and four horses were uncovered in the dromos. The chariots resemble those depicted on 14th century BC Mycenaean *craters*. (type of bowl)

Two asses and a chariot were found in the dromos of *tomb 2*, along with evidence of human sacrifice.

Cellarka

Continuing along the narrow and rough tarmac road from the Royal Tombs, after a few hundred yards, a turnoff to the left will be seen, leading up to an area enclosed by a wire mesh fence. Within is an extraordinary hive of cells carved from the rock. It is, in fact, a complex of tombs, like miniatures of the Royal Tombs, and reminiscent of the much earlier Bronze Age necropolis of Vounous. The workmanship is excellent, and the way in which the multitude of cells is fitted together is

CELLARKA TOMB   SECTION OF AQUEDUCT

quite remarkable. The dromoi have steps rather than slopes, and sometimes lead to a pair of chambers. Some of the tombs have a low plinth for the occupant. Heavy stone doors once sealed the entrances.

AYIOS BARNABAS MONASTERY

Barnabas, along with Mark and Paul, founded the orthodox apostolic church of Cyprus. The patriarchate of Antioch claimed authority over the church, but the issue was finally settled during the term of office of Anthemios, archbishop of Cyprus, in 488 AD. Tradition relates that the location of the tomb of Barnabas was revealed to Anthemios in a dream.

113

The apostle was found in his tomb with a copy of the gospel of St.Matthew on his breast, placed there by St.Mark. Anthemios proceeded to Constantinople where he presented the document to Emperor Zeno. Duly impressed, the emperor confirmed the autocephalus status of the church of Cyprus, and further, granted the archbishop the imperial privelege of officiating in purple, of carrying a sceptre in place of the pastoral staff, and of signing documents in red ink, customs maintained to this day.

The church itself is a reconstruction (1756) of a forerunner dating from the 10th century, and is of little architectural interest. A few capitals built into the wall, and a green marble column are all that remain of the early Byzantine building. This column is supposed to exude a liquid which alleviates eye problems and other illnesses.

A short distance from the cloister is the catacomb where Archbishop Anthemios is said to have discovered the relics of St.Barnabas. The tomb of Barnabas is still a place of pilgrimage for those Greek Cypriots who remain in the north of the island.

Icon and Archeological Museum

Housed in the church is an extensive collection of painted and gilt icons, both ancient and modern. The cloisters have recently been renovated, and converted into an archeological museum containing artifacts spanning the gulf between Neolithic and Roman times. Of particular interest are the exceptional specimens of Bronze Age pottery.

A visit to this museum is highly recommended: it is well laid out so that even a casual perusal will reveal the development and stylistic changes in pottery design as the succession of cultural waves washed across the island down the centuries. Regrettably, the provenance of the exhibits is not included on the labels.

Toilet facilities are available in the museum. There is also a snack bar, and a gift shop. Open every day from 9am until 6pm.

The Cenotaph of Nicocreon

In 1965 a large tumulus (150 ft across by 30 ft high) was excavated by Dr.V.Karageorghis for the Cyprus Department of Antiquities. Situated in the village of Tuzla (Engomi), this tumulus had been tunnelled in the past by various treasure seekers who were deceived into thinking that any

114

remains would be in the middle. Karageorghis discovered a platform or exedra some 55ft by 35ft, well off centre, surmounted by a pyramid of rocks. Under these rocks was a layer of mud bricks, beneath which was revealed the remains of a pyre. Amongst the ashes and charcoal were found numerous objects, including gilt clay pots, and fragments of clay figures, but no human remains, indicating that this is a cenotaph. The figures were formed on wooden poles which were inserted into holes arranged around the pyre. Some of the figures had distinctive features, suggesting that they may be images of real people. The style of the figures date the cenotaph to the end of the 4th century BC, which coincides with the time of Nicocreon, the last king of Salamis.

The inheritance of Alexander the Great was disputed by Ptolemy and Antigonus, each of whom claimed Cyprus as part of his fief. Ptolemy eventually gained the ascendancy, and Nicocreon, who had conspired with Antigonus, was forced to commit suicide along with all his family. It is surmised that the royal family gathered within, and fired their palace, which collapsed over them. In their honour, the Salaminians erected a cenotaph, and perhaps the clay figures represent members of the royal family.

The remains, a stepped platform surrounded by piles of rubbish, are of scant interest, and belie the archaeological importance of this site.

Enkomi

The road from Salamis to Ayios Barnabas continues on to the ruins of Enkomi. In spring this route is exquisitely decorated with wayside flowers, including poppies, yellow daisies and borage, which follow the earlier narcissi and anemones. In summer, hardy clumps of thyme show their colours, resembling small purple boulders when seen from a distance.

The site was originally held to be a necropolis, and several tombs were excavated by the British, (in 1896), and the Swedish, (in 1930), before Professor Schaeffer discovered in 1934 that Enkomi was in fact a town where the dead were entombed in the courtyards of the houses.

Archaeological traces in Enkomi date back to the beginning of the 2nd millenium BC, but it was not until the expulsion of the Hyksos from the eastern Mediterranean by the Pharaohs of the 18th dynasty that the town developed and flourished.

The Egyptian El Amarna tablets, which record correspondence between foreign rulers and the Pharaohs, refer several times to the

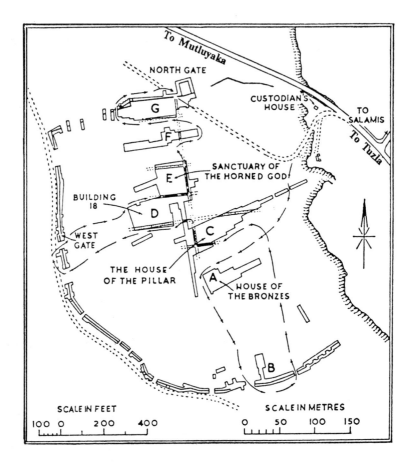

ENKOMI - PLAN VIEW

payment of tribute in copper by the king of Alasia. Some scholars identify Alasia with Cyprus, or indeed with Enkomi itself, as it is clear that this town was an important trading centre at this time, and was working and exporting copper to various countries in the near east.

After the 14th century BC, the Achaeans began to settle in Cyprus, and their influence can be seen the Mycenaean pottery found in contemporary tombs of Enkomi. Other tomb finds include gold jewellery, items of ivory, cylinder seals and bronze ware.

Excavations reveal that the town was destroyed towards the end of the 13th century BC, and rebuilt shortly after according to a new layout.

Massive city walls were erected, and the streets were laid out in a regular grid system. Large public buildings were constructed from ashlar blocks, and the central town square was paved with stone slabs. Two sanctuaries have been uncovered, in one of which was found a 21 inch high bronze statue of a god wearing a horned headpiece.

Subsequent destruction of the town has been attributed to the *sea people*, and despite an influx of new settlers from the Levant and the Aegean, Enkomi never recovered, and its fate was sealed by an earthquake in 1075 BC.

Description

A: The House of the Bronzes, so called after the numerous bronze artifacts discovered there.

B: Part of the city wall was excavated in this area, consisting of two rows of large stone blocks, the gap between being filled with rubble. The remains of a watch tower can be seen in the eastern section of the wall.

C: In this residential area of the wealthy, tombs have yielded treasures of gold, silver, and fine Mycenaean pottery. Here is located the *House of the Pillar*, a sanctuary whose roof was supported by a stone pillar.

D: Building 18, once a two storey structure, consists of two wings, with a rectangular inner courtyard. Built from large ashlar blocks and dating from the 14th century bc, this house shows Mycenaean influence, and is assumed to have been the residence of an Achaean prince. The bronze statue of the horned god was found amongst these ruins.

E: In the *Sanctuary of the Horned God*, a further statuette was discovered, along with remains of animal sacrifice. To the east are workshops where copper was worked.

F: In this area, many bronze articles were unearthed, including a sceptre.

G: This region, bounded in the north by the city wall, was the main site of the copper industry.

THE KARPAS PENINSULAR

Largely undiscovered by the tourist, the Karpas peninsular is replete with antique towns, tombs, temples and basilicas from all the different periods, and was once a thickly populated region. The geographer Strabo refers to the towns of Urania, Aphrodisium, and Carpasia, but so far only Carpasia can be identified.

Teucer, the founder of Salamis, is supposed to have first landed on the *Achaeans Beach*, to the north of Yeni Erenköy (Yialousa).

In the Middle Ages, the Karpas was one of the largest baronies under the Lusignans.

The tourist is strongly recommended to spend at least two days of his holiday visiting the Karpas. Convenient accommodation may be found at the Blue Sea hotel, located three or four miles beyond Dipkarpas.

Iskele (Trikomo)

This village is known for its pomegranates and its diminutive Dominican church of **Ayios Iakovos**, which stands in the village square. In the nearby church of Panayia Theotokos, paintings from the 12th and 15th centuries can be seen. (see below) Trikomo is also the birthplace of the notorious terrorist George Grivas.

Panayia Theotokos

This Byzantine building with its outstanding frescoes of the early Comnenian style, was built in the early 12th century as a single aisled, domed church. In the 15th century a vaulted aisle was added to the north side. Set into the modern belfry is a remarkable carved marble stone (thorakion), which came from the original iconostasis (altar screen) of the church.

In the cupola, Christ Pantocrator is depicted surrounded by a choir of worshipping angels on bended knee, and with hands outstretched under their *himations.*(Upper garment wrapped around the body, leaving part of the breast free - worn by Christ, the Apostles, and some saints.) These angels, headed by two archangels wearing the *loros*, (Imperial embroidered and bejewelled cloth of gold worn by the ushers to the Byzantine court) approach the Preparation of the Throne from each side; the throne itself is flanked by the Virgin Mary, and John the Baptist. The

118

scene is an interesting example of the interrelation between Imperial court customs and Byzantine iconography.

In other parts of the building are frescoes revealing the life of the Virgin Mary, according to the apocryphal gospels. In the conch of the apse is a finely executed *Mary Orans*, a 15th century repainting of the *Mary Blachernitissa* type of monumental painting. In the north aisle can be seen Franco - Byzantine murals of the 15th century.

At Sinirüstü (Syngrasis), two miles west of İskele, the large 13th century church of **Ayios Prokopios** retains some features including opus sectile flooring in the apse, murals of the saint and a Byzantine inscription. Near the community hall one arch of **Ayios Nikolaos** stands amidst debris.

KANTARA

Shortly before Boğaz, a junction in the coastal road leads inland via Yarköy (Ayios Elias) and Turnalar (Yerani), and on up to the village of Kantara. The castle lies about 3 miles further to the east. Access is also possible from the north coast road, via Kaplıca (Dhavlos).

History:

Kantara castle was built in the 10th century as a lookout post, and was remodelled by the Lusignans in the 12th century.

The name Kantara is derived from the Arabic word meaning bridge or arch, and certainly the castle does bridge the range, commanding views in all directions from its altitude of 2000 ft.

The castle is first mentioned in connection with Richard the Lionheart's conquest of the island.The tyrant ruler of Cyprus, Isaac Comnenos, fled to Kantara after his defeat in battle, but later surrendered, and was brought before Richard bound in silver chains.

In 1229, supporters of Emperor Frederick II retired to Kantara after being defeated by the forces of Jean d'Ibelin, whose property they had tried to confiscate. They eventually surrendered when faced with starvation in the summer of 1230.

When the Genoese overran the island in 1373, Kantara remained in Lusignan hands, and was the refuge of the Prince of Antioch, uncle to Peter II. The latter, captured and humiliated by the Genoese in Famagusta, succeeded in escaping to Kantara while disguised as a cook's scullion by his faithful servant and cook, Galentiri.

119

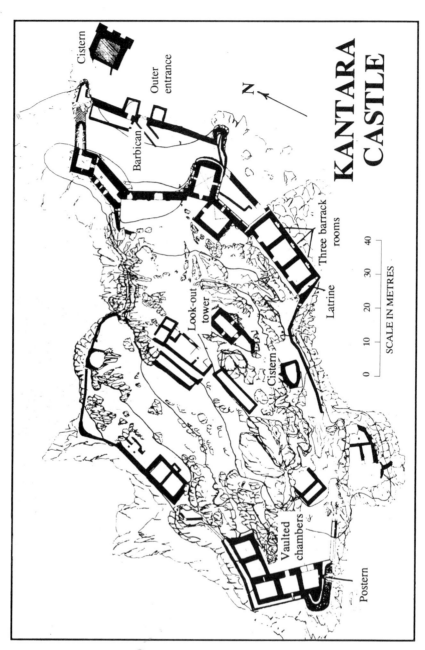

KANTARA CASTLE - PLAN VIEW

The castle was fortified by James I (1382-1398), and continued to be an important stronghold until it was abandoned and partially dismantled by the Venetians in 1525.

Description:

Planted upon steep cliffs, the castle is virtually impregnable, and extra fortification of the entrance further reduced possible forced entry.

KANTARA CASTLE: A VIEW FROM THE SOUTH-EAST

The barbican, flanked by a pair of square towers, leads into a large bailey, an area between the outer and the main wall. Piercing this wall is the inner entrance, protected by two towers which survive in good condition. The north-east tower is a two storey structure fitted with shooting slits. In the south-east tower is a rectangular room which the crusader knights used as a prison. Adjoining the tower are three vaulted rooms with shooting slits, where the knights stayed.

The path to the south leads past a cistern and a ruined tower to a complex of vaulted rooms, and the latrines. Various other rooms and cisterns can be seen, but little remains of the north-west part of the castle.

121

It is worth climbing up to the highest point of the castle which affords excellent views, particularly along the chain of the Kyrenia range. Flares were used to signal to Buffavento castle and Nicosia during the night.

Large *griffon vultures* can often be seen soaring about the heights of Kantara and the surrounding mountains.

Sazlıköy (Livadia)

This village lies about 3 miles to the north of Çayırova, (Ayios Theodoros) and a few hundred yards further stands the little Byzantine church of **Panayia Kyras**. In the earlier apse, which was incorporated into the church, the remains of a 6th century mosaic of the Virgin Mary can be found. Locals believed that the mosaic cubes were effective against minor ailments, which accounts for the virgin's vanishing act. Patches of 13th century murals remain in the church.

In the vicinity of the church are remnants of a late Roman and Byzantine town.

Nitovikla

Four miles south of Kuruova (Korovia), on a cliff which plunges sheer into the sea, are the ruins of the fortress of Nitovikla, which dates from

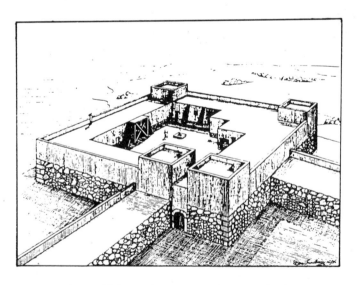

FORTRESS OF NITOVIKLA - A RECONSTRUCTION

the Middle Bronze Age. Two towers guarded the entrance to a large compound surrounded by massive walls. It is assumed that this was a safe retreat for villagers in the outlying district in times of conflict.

There are similarities between this structure and the fortress in Boğazköy on the Anatolian mainland.

Boltaşlı (Lythrangomi)

The road from Çayırova (Ayios Theodoros) passes through Pamuklu (Tavros), Kumyalı (Koma tou Yialou) and on to Ziyamet, where it branches off to Boltaşlı. Situated on the far side of the village is the church of **Panayia Kanakaria**.

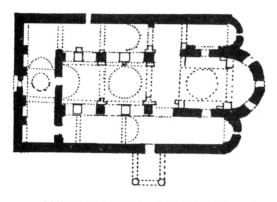

PANAYIA KANAKARIA - GROUND PLAN

Erected in 1160, this church incorporated the apse of an early Christian basilica which once occupied the site. The narthex, and the small porch on the south side are later additions which incorporate some columns and corinthian capitals from the original building. The principal attraction of the church, a mosaic of the Virgin and Child was recently removed from the apse by art thieves. In the lunette above the south portal, a fresco in the 16th century Italian style can be seen.

In the immediate vicinity of the church are fragments of the early Byzantine basilica, a flour mill, and evidence that a large Byzantine town was once located here.

The Sepulchres at Elisis and Kaleburnu (Galinporni)

From Boltaşlı, the road continues on through Derince (Vathylakkas) and Avtepe (Ayios Symeon). Proceeding in the direction of Kuruova

(Korovia), the road runs below a high ridge on the right hand side. A couple of miles out of Avtepe, the keen observer will spot a dark patch in the cliff above. This marks the entrance to an enormous man made cave comprising a nave, and two aisles with lateral sepulchral chambers. A ladder and a torch are the minimum requirements for visiting this site, and most visitors will pass on to Kaleburnu, where the tomb is more accessible. At the east side of the village, the road climbs and then passes to the right of a hill in a track which leads down into the valley. About a hundred yards along this track a very narrow path descends the steep face of the hill until the entrance of the cave is gained. Once again, a torch is essential for inspecting the depths of the sepulchre.

Hogarth, who has described these tombs in detail in his *Devia Cypria,* concludes that they are Phoenician in style, and may date from the 5th or 4th century BC.

Ayia Trias

This 6th century columnar basilica is situated on the left hand side of the road which leads from the hamlet of Sipahi (Ayia Trias) to the north coast road. A rusting bus (a later addition) shares the site. The entrance portals of this three aisled basilica were preceded by a narthex, which opened on to a peristyle atrium. In the middle of the nave are the remains of a once richly ornamented chancel. An inscription in front of the main apse records one Diacon Heraclios as a benefactor of the church. Extensive areas of mosaic paving survive: these are mainly geometric in design, but note the thistles represented in the north aisle, and the charming pair of sandals which symbolize pilgrimage. The mosaics were produced locally but reflect the artistic trends of the eastern Mediterranean, especially of Antioch, one of the main centres of mosaic production. There is a baptistry to the south east of the eastern processional type, similar to that at Ayios Philon, and remains of the marble-clad steps, which led down to the font sunk in the floor, can be seen. The bishop's palace was located to the west of the church.

There are three churches of interest along the north coast road from Ayia Trias to Dipkarpaz. The first is **Ayios Thyrsos**, easily located near the shore behind its large white neo-gothic successor. This small barrel vaulted church has a transverse arch resting on corbels; the corbel between the two interior arches is plain, but the other, above the doorway, features an incised supportive hand in the design. Steps inside the left hand arch lead to an *ayiasma*, or holy well. The second is the double aisled church of **Ayios Photios tis Selinias,** set back from the road about two miles further on. The dome of this 10th century building is rather flat, and the drum on which it rests is not circular. There is evidence of an additional north aisle. In the conch of the apse is a Mary Orans of the Blachernitissa style, and on the walls are remains of Franco-byzantine murals. Surrounding the church are potshards, millstones and large ashlar blocks, indicative of an ancient settlement in this area. Two miles further on, the third church, **Panayia Eleousa** (Our Lady of Pity) may be reached by following the rough track which leads off at an acute angle just after the road bends sharply to the right. After about a mile, a few abandoned modern buildings come into view. The small two aisled 15th century Byzantine church, lying behind the ruins on the left, shows some Gothic elements. Dog-tooth moulding decorates the attractive south-facing doorway.

Dipkarpaz (Rizokarpaso)

The several villages in this district were built in Byzantine times from the ruins of ancient Carpasia, a couple of miles to the north. During the ascendency of the latin church, Rizokarpaso was the seat of the orthodox bishop of Famagusta.

The 12th century church of **Ayios Synesios,** which shows architectural details and decorative elements copied from the cathedrals in Nicosia and Famagusta, was enlarged in the 18th century. The church, situated in the town centre, is still used by the Greek Cypriots still living in the Karpas.

Carpasia

Two miles to the north of Dipkarpaz lie the ruins of the old harbour town of Carpasia, which was probably founded by either the Achaeans or the Phoenicians.

In 306 BC, Demetrius, a son of one of the successors to Alexander the Great, Antigonus, landed in force near Carpasia, and took the town by surprise. Demetrius subsequently subjugated the entire island, remaining in possession for 10 years until expelled by Ptolemy. Carpasia had a good artificial harbour with two moles made of stone blocks fastened together with metal clamps.

It is recorded that in the 3rd century BC the Carpasians took part in the pan Athenian games.

125

In the 4th century AD, Carpasia became the seat of a bishop. It is said that Pulcheria, sister to Emperor Arkadius, fell ill and sent her deacon, Philon, to Epiphanios, the bishop of Salamis, who was celebrated for his powers of healing. Before embarking on his mission to Rome, Epiphanios ordained Philon as the first bishop of Carpasia.

The town was destroyed by saracens in the 9th century AD, and abandoned by its inhabitants. All that remains are a few stone walls, the harbour moles, and the ruins of Ayios Philon Basilica. To the west of the town are rock cut tombs from Hellenistic and Roman times.

Ayios Philon

This early 5th century complex consists of a basilica, a peristyle court, a bishop's palace, and sundry buildings. These were built on the foundations of earlier Hellenistic and Roman structures. The basilica, which was some thirty yards long, consisted of three aisles, with a narthex to the east. The far end of the peristyle atrium beyond the narthex has long since been claimed by the sea. The irregular spacing between the columns leads to the conclusion that Ayios Philon, like the

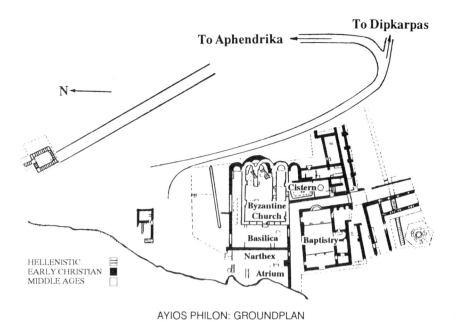

AYIOS PHILON: GROUNDPLAN

126

basilica of Soli, was an architrave structure, wherein the columns were joined by beams, rather than by arches. To the southeast, in the baptistry, are the remnants of a marble mosaic floor, including a large circular work similar to that at Kampanopetra in Salamis. The eastern processionary type font was formerly clad in marble.

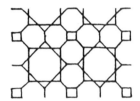 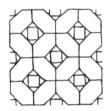 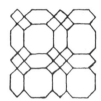

OPUS SECTILE FLOOR PATTERNS

In the 12th century, a domed Byzantine church was erected on the site of the early Christian basilica. The Byzantine technique of placing a dome on four linked arches is clearly demonstrated at this site.

Aphendrika

Four miles further east is the site of Aphendrika, which was, according to Strabo, one of the six major cities of Cyprus in the 3rd century BC. Remains of a citadel and tombs from Hellenistic times can be seen, and a mile to the north, traces of the ancient harbour can be recognized.

The first ruins on the left are of the domed Byzantine church of Ayios Yeoryios (St.George), built at the turn of the 10th century. It has a double apse, with niches on either side. The rounded-square drum under the now fallen dome rested on arches linking the four piers just west of the apses - a Byzantine solution evolved for placing a dome on a square plan.

The ruined basilicas of Asomatos and Panayia date from the 6th century, but the original wooden roofs were replaced with barrel vaulting after their destruction by Arabs at the end of the 10th century. Characteristic features are the blind arcading and the absence of clerestory windows.

Panayia, the church next to Ayios Yeoryios, was again destroyed in medieval times, and rebuilt in the 16th century. This building, with its pointed barrel vaulting, occupies only a part of the nave of the former basilica. Of the rest of the basilica, wall sections of the south aisle and the foundations of the apses are still visible. The colonnade structure of the original basilica has been determined from the column remaining *in situ* in the first arch of the south wall (see inset photograph), and half-column fragments which terminated the colonnade at the western extremity and in the apse.

The Asomatos basilica, across the prickly scrub to the right, preserves more features, including apsidial passages (also discernible in the Panayia) and intact vaulting over the south aisle. Careful examination reveals that the nave arcades do not bond with the apse - these arcades replaced the original colonnades when the vaulting was added.

COLUMN FROM ORIGINAL BASILICA

A mile or so further down the track to the east, past the first rocky outcrop, a hill may be seen on the right hand side. On this was built the citadel of the early pre-christian city which once existed here. The rooms were partly excavated into the rock, but no masonry survives of the upper sections of wall. Carved into the hillside at various levels are tombs, and some large chambers with smoke holes in the middle of the ceilings.

Apostolos Andreas

According to legend, St.Andrew was on his way back to Palestine on ship whose captain was blind in one eye. They put in for water: St.Andrew struck the rock where the monastery now stands, and out gushed a spring, the magic properties of which restored the captains sight.

The monastery, which served to accommodate both Moslem and Christian pilgrims, is a relatively recent structure. Below it, next to the sea, is the 15th century chapel. A single central pillar supports the vaulting of this chamber. In one corner is a spring which served as the *ayiasma*: its waters may be sampled outside the chapel on the seaward side.

Three miles to the north at Zafer Burnu (Cape Apostolos Andreas), a few stones remain of the temple to Aphrodite Akraia. At the tip of the cape, Neolithic remains of Kastros were excavated in 1973.

FOLKART IN CYPRUS

For thousands of years Cyprus has been snatched up by successive regional powers eager to exploit the timber and mineral resources of the island. Conquest brings in its wake the culture of the conquerors, and for many centuries, local artists and artisans have been able to draw from a wide variety of cultural sources.

Oriental and occidental traditions combine to form a rich synthesis in design and decoration evident in the pottery, weaving and woodcarving of the islanders.

Weaving

Embroideries, woven into household linen and blankets, were common in almost every Cypriot village early this century, and the art is still practiced in some parts of the Mesaoria and in the Karpas. The designs, impressive in their arrangement of patterns, and combination of colours, reveal the influence of 16th century Venetian embroideries. Exquisite lace was, and to a limited extent still is, produced, and according to tradition, Leonardo da Vinci visited Lefkara (S.Cyprus) to order lace for the altar of Milan Cathedral.

The raw materials for weaving - cotton, linen, silk and wool - were formerly important agricultural products of Cyprus. Cotton and silk were of the first quality, and had a good reputation in the markets of Europe. The finest and whitest silk came from Famagusta and the Karpas. The lemon sulphur coloured silk preferred by the Turks, came from Değirmenlik (Kythrea) and villages on the northern slopes of the Kyrenia range.The silk industry has now vanished except for a few villages in the Karpas. Mulberry trees, on which leaves the silk worms feed, are a common sight along the north coast. Cotton is still woven in some villages, again in the Karpas and Mesaoria.

Pottery

Skilled potters still work at wheels little changed over the centuries except for the addition of a small electric motor. The clay found in in certain areas around Lapta and Famagusta is especially suitable for wheel made glazed pottery. However, apart from some custom made items for restaurants and bars, everyday wares are no longer produced, and the traditional incised and painted designs decorate vases and bowls which are destined to adorn the tourists table.

Woodcarving

Traditional village wood carving has almost died out, and few examples of carved wooden furniture remain. Built in shelves and wall cupboards still exist in some of the old style houses, but much of the moveable furniture, particularly the massive chests, have been acquired by collectors. The chests were used to store household linen, and were often a part of the brides dowry. They are usually carved with geometric patterns and floral designs, sometimes with stylised animal and human figures engraved or in relief. Most of the chests are constructed from Cyprus walnut, a hard, durable wood, but pine was also used. Some are painted in red, blue and green colours.

The best examples of traditional carving were found on the iconostasis (altar screen) in the Byzantine churches. Unfortunately vandals have destroyed many of these, but it is still possible to see this craftsmanship in the Monastery of Ayios Mamas in Güzelyurt (Morphou), Bellapais Abbey, in the church at Karmi, and St. Barnabas Monastery (near Salamis).

Cane baskets have not yet been entirely displaced by the ubiquitous plastic bag (known here as 'nylon'), and locally made baskets in all shapes and sizes are available in most markets.

Music

Turkish Cypriot folk music has its origin in ancient Anatolian music, and instruments typical of that area can also be found in N. Cyprus. The *davul*, a two headed resonant cylindrical drum, is usually used to accompany the *zurna*. The *darbuka* is an oriental skin covered clay pitcher, which is also common from the Balkans to Afghanistan, and from the Caucasus to Arabic Africa. The zurna is a conical, double reed, shrill voiced member of the oboe family, usually with seven finger holes plus one thumb hole. It is played with the reed inside the mouth.

In the string section are the *saz*, a long necked lute with a pear shaped body which comes in several sizes: the small *cura sazı* (three stringed), the middle sized - and most commonly used - *bağlama* (six stringed), the *bozuk* (eight stringed), and the large *divan sazı* (twelve stringed). The *keman*, a small violin played in a vertical position resting on the players knee or thigh, and the banjo shaped *cumbus* complete this group.

Turkish shepherds often play the *dilliduduk*, a vertical flute about 30 - 40 cm long, with five or six finger holes plus one thumb hole.

Folk music plays an important role in social, cultural and religious life. The tunes, categorized as dance tunes, wedding music, work songs, religious and historical songs, reflect the traditional, historical and religious background of the Turkish Cypriot people.

Ceremonies

The visitor in August will soon be aware that this is the month of marriage. With horns blaring, carloads, and even busloads of relatives and friends attend the ceremony, and the subsequent feast. It is customary to pin currency notes to the dress of the bride and groom. Arranged marriages are still common, though many of the younger generation prefer to choose for themselves.

Another ceremony which the visitor may witness concerns the circumcision of boys *(sünnet)*, usually at the age of about eight. On the day of this rite, the boy is dressed up in colourful attire and led through the city, town or village on a horse with bright trappings. The green banner of Islam precedes him, and the musicians, family and friends all follow him to the mosque, where a prayer is said. The procession then goes back to the house where the operation is performed by an expert. Presents are given, followed by a great feast.

FLORA AND FAUNA

Forestry

There is evidence that in ancient times much of the island of Cyprus was thickly covered with forests of pine, cypress and cedar. It was certainly richer in timber than the Phoenician coast and Egypt, and this resource, along with the abundant copper deposits, attracted the attention of neighbouring powers.

Since the Stone Age, man has recognized the remarkable utility of wood. When burnt, it provided warmth and light, heat for cooking, and the dancing flames scared away wild animals. As a building material - light and strong, and easily worked - it had no equal. The only problem was that demand soon exceeded renewable supply. Surrounding countries plundered Cypriot forests to build their ships, intensive copper mining operations encroached upon the forests, and used large quantities of wood for pit props and smelting, whilst careless use of fire accounted for periodic mass destruction. Clearance for crop production was encouraged in ancient times, and the decimation continued until the British occupation in 1878. During the war, the forests were heavily felled to supply the Allied Forces in the Middle East - this was selective and regulative, but much time is required for regrowth. The loss of forest cover has adversely affected the water table, and the substantial rivers which once flowed in the island have dried up, or degenerated into winter rivulets.

The Forestry Department is doing its best to redress the situation with the limited resources at its disposal, and there has been some success with their replanting projects.

Some of the principal species are listed below.

Pinus Brutia Most common and commercially important species - very resinous - in earlier days was tapped for resin (pitch wood in Turkish times). Used for making fruit boxes and general constructional purposes. A medium grade tanning material is extracted from the bark.

Cypress Found mostly on the Kyrenia range but also scattered about the plains, where it is used as a windbreak. Two varieties - one tall and slim, the other rather ragged. Commonly used as rafters in certain types of village house.

Cypress trees grew, and were worshipped in Cyprus since ancient times, and some claim that they take their name from the island. In classical times they were sacred to Pluto - emblems of grief and eternity, and are often found in graveyards.

Stone Pine Introduced into the island many years ago, possibly in Roman times. Grows well at most levels, but chiefly used in reclamation work at sea level, as in Salamis. Useful for general constructional puposes, it is best known for its edible seeds - *pinolia* - commonly used in confectionary all over the Mediterranean.

Eucalyptus Numerous species have been introduced from Australia. Used for shipbuilding, furniture and posts. Found mainly in the Nicosia area, but also scattered along the lower reaches of the north coast.

Several other species are used to make furniture, including the *Walnut and Plane.* The unripe fruit of the walnut is often candied, and served with Turkish coffee to guests.

Olive Indigenous to Cyprus - must be grafted to produce good fruit. An mportant agricultural crop pickled in brine, or processed into oil. The wood makes excellent charcoal, and is a first rate fuel.

Carob Indigenous to Cyprus, the wild carob must be budded to produce a commercially useful crop. A black syrup (Pekmez) extracted from the crushed large black beans, is used as a substitute for sugar in confectionary. Carobs are also used as an animal fodder. Cyprus is reputed to grow the best quality pods in the world, and this crop was once the most valuable export of the island, earning the name *'the black gold of Cyprus'*. The carobs were stored in large stone warehouses by the shore, from where they were loaded into ships. Many of the restaurants lining Kyrenia harbour are converted carob warehouses, and many more can be seen along the coast road to the Karpas, monuments to a by-gone age.

The seeds of the carob are extremely hard, and of fairly uniform weight. They were originally used as the jeweller's carat (4 grains).

Almond Extensively cultivated, this deciduous tree bursts into flower in the early spring, transforming villages such as Bellapais and Karaman

(Karmi) with their pink and white blossom. The wild variety is bitter, containing traces of poisonous prussic acid. The nuts are harvested in late summer.

Citrus Known colloquially as 'lemons'. Many varieties are grown from the Kyrenia district to Güzelyurt (Morphou). Oranges, lemons, grapefruit and tangerines are a very important export crop, harvested around Christmas time. Juice is also extracted and packed in cartons. Bitter (Seville) orange trees (the basic stock on to which other varieties are grafted) are often grown ornamentally in gardens and elsewhere, the orange fruit making an attractive show against the dark green foliage. Occasionally trees may be seen bearing both oranges and lemons - a matter of grafting. Bitter oranges are also used by British expatriates to make marmalade.

Fig Widespread, grows up to 15 feet when cultivated, or a scrambling shrub when semi wild. The fruit is eaten fresh; also used medicinally. Note the very old *Ficus Sycomorus* tree outside Famagusta Cathedral, which is a different species, but which bears fruit resembling tiny figs. This is the sycomore fig mentioned in the bible; it is not native to Cyprus, and this particular tree was undoubtedly planted on purpose at this location.

Other fruit trees found include the *Pomegranate, loquat, mulberry, apricot, damson, mosphilo, date palm, and banana.*

Of these, the *mulberry*, originating from China, is a relic of the silk industry, and the *loquat* is a hardy import from Japan, bearing small yellow fruit with four large seeds.

Flowers of Cyprus

The brilliant and varied display of wild flowers which the visitor beholds in February, March and April begins to build up after the Autumn rains have given a good wetting to the soil, beginning with tiny *grape hyacinth* and *narcissi*, and climaxing in February and March with *cyclamen* and the many coloured *anemones* painting the fields in blue, red, pink and white. A miniature *iris* and wild *gladioli* also abound. The verges of road and field are full of the tall *asphodel*, best left unpicked, as they smell of tomcats. Olive orchards stand in lakes of acid-yellow *oxalis*, or blood red *poppies*, dazzling in the sunlight. Waste areas are carpeted with the *golden crown daisy* (or wild *chrysanthemum*), often with the creamy, many branched *scabious*. The dark red *Cyprus tulip* is prolific in some

134

western parts. Soon the fists of the *giant fennel* (some are ten feet tall) unfurl their feathery foliage and large yellow flower heads.

It was hidden in the dry pithy stem of this fennel that Prometheus was said to have brought to men the fire stolen from heaven. A special sight is the giant fennel pushing out of the grassy waste in front of the drooping fronds of the *acacias* to the right of the road from Famagusta to Salamis.

On the hillsides the *rock roses*, purple, pink and white, along with other flowering and aromatic shrubs, bloom over several months. Parasitic on the roots of the rock rose is the brilliant yellow *Cytinus*, its buds enclosed in scarlet scales, a solid clump of colour - worth looking out for. Those clumps of 'barbed wire', which are the dormant *spiny burnet* bushes, suddenly green all over and acquire their white, pink, then red glistening berries. Gradually the soft new twigs harden up, and become the pale 'barbed wire'. The matted twigs are often used as brooms, and for firing the ovens - it seems this has gone on since Biblical times (Eccles.VII.6).

Around March/April, also, quite a few wild *orchids* flourish on rocky stretches near the seaside, and among grassy patches explored from the mountain roads. These months also witness the brilliant yellow masses of the *prickly broom*, swarming in the valleys, and the lower slopes of the mountains, redolent with the heavy scent of honey.

As the Summer approaches, the colourful *echiums* and other silver leaved plants appear, often still twined with the pink *convulvulus*, and three or four *mallows*. The soils in this region, dominated by the limestone hills of the Kyrenia range, are largely alkaline, and acid loving plants are absent.

Even in the long rainless Summer, flowers are to be found, especially a succession of attractive *thistles* - pale yellow, purple, pink, royal blue, and bronze. Some form prickly electric-blue mats, some densely flowered mounds, while others tower six feet above the ground. The local *thyme* makes stiff twigged, aromatic hummocks, and the gorgeous white flowers of the thorny *caper* bush, with their swirl of purple stamens, scent the evening air. *Myrtles* grow along the wadis, which are often full of the pink flowered, fragrant *oleander* bushes, and feathery *tamarisk*, while pungent *lentisc* and *terebinth* grow in rocky corners.

135

Very frequent on the slopes of the hills is the *Arbutus*, or strawberry tree, lovely at every season. The new branches are crimson barked, the leaves glossy green; clusters of creamy bells in the spring are followed by strawberry-like edible fruits.

Standing out from rocky wastes can usually be seen one or two *Giant Agaves* in flower. The central stem rises from the cluster of thick, sword-like leaves to a height of up to thirty feet, in a matter of days. This plant takes 10 - 15 years to flower, and then dies, so many dried up half fallen stems are always visible.

The ultimate in hardiness is displayed by the *Giant Squill*, whose leafless stalk shoots up out of the parched earth in July/August, and the tall spikes of pale starry flowers, in the morning or evening light, seem like a procession of ghosts over the waste land. At the same season the fringed white flowers of the *sea daffodil* burst improbably from the dunes in many places, breathing a heavy perfume into the evening breeze.

'Street' trees are often spectacular. You can take your coffee under superb *Jacarandas*, shedding a bright mauve mat on the ground, opposite the Law Courts in Kyrenia. In front of the Police Station is a *Persian lilac*, with its black eyed lilac blooms. Lacy-leaved *Parkinsonias* bloom twice a year, yellow with orange/red flowers which drop to form a carpet under their spreading, shady branches. Especially in the neighbourhood of the sea, *rubber plants* thrive, of a size you would never get into your house. In the villages, black, and white *mulberries* feed people (fruit), pets and silkworms (leaves). The golden oriole, a visitor to Cyprus, is also rather partial to the berries. Purple flowered *Judas* trees, erupting at Easter, and the deep pink and mauve-trumpeted flowers of the *Bauhinia* last for ages on the tree, which is afterwards dripping with long thin bean pods.

Birds of Cyprus

The greater part of the bird population is migratory, and includes many species commonly seen in the British Isles - *finches, warblers, swallows, tits, martins, robins, blackbirds* etc. Some migrants pass right through, some rest a while, and others occasionally stay on for a summer or winter sojourn. Very many of these small birds are caught on lime-sticks, or in nets, and eaten. It may be of interest to note a few of the more exotic species.

In March and April, *cranes* may be observed flying North, high up, in their shaggy V's. They return South in August - October, and huge flocks can be seen and heard coming in over Kyrenia and Güzelyurt, arriving from Turkey in vast 'V' formations. Over St.Hilarion and Buffavento they can be seen circling to catch the thermals to give them the height to move on to the next stop. Flocks of *storks* may appear then too, and very occasionally one will be found resting here. In August/September, flocks of glossy *ibis* occasionally pass along the North coast; *buzzards* fly over in large numbers to Africa, and one or two stop off on rare occasions.

Of the spring migrants, some of the *swallows* - ordinary and red-rumped varieties - stay to breed, as do the *swifts*, very visible in the towns and harbours. Some of the chestnut-backed, bright blue *rollers*, seen engagingly turning off the telegraph wires, also stay to breed (April/May), as do the *masked shrike*. The sweetly chirruping and gorgeously coloured *bee-eaters* mostly pass through in spring and autumn, staying for a month or so, like the *golden orioles*, with their clear musical whistle, and purposeful flight. Another distinctive voiced Summer visitor is the smart pink, black, and white *hoopoe*. *Kingfishers* are migrants too, but can be seen any time of year, dipping into the sea in a quiet cove, or poised over a large water tank, beady-eyeing the 'mosquito fish' therein.

It is worth visiting the reservoirs at Gönyeli and Geçitköy, especially during winter, when many *ducks* (see the mosaics in Soli) - *wigeon, teal, shoveler* etc. are visitors, as well as the beautiful *hen harrier* and *marsh harrier*. *Grey herons* and *egrets* are also in evidence.

Resident birds include the little dark speckled Cyprus *warbler*, and the grey and pinky-brown spectacled warbler. Common *crows*, which wear grey waistcoats in Cyprus, are found in every field. There are several owls, including the very round *little owl*, and the long (7") narrow *Scops owl*, the soft call and response of the latter being a delight to hear in the cool of the evening.

Occasionally the almost extinct *griffon vulture* may be seen soaring along the Kyrenia range, especially at Kantara. Another rarity is the handsome black partridge or *francolin*, while the red legged Cyprus *chukor* is abundant and vocal, strikingly striped in black and chestnut.

The bird watcher will have no difficulty in adding to this necessarily abbreviated list, and will find a European bird guide a useful companion.

Beasts of Cyprus

The range of wild animals found in Cyprus falls far short of the spectrum of birds to be seen. The visitor may count himself lucky if he sees a moufflon - a symbol of Cyprus - in captivity, let alone in the wild. The indigenous species of cow still exists, and attempts are being made to preserve it in an animal park in Çatalköy. Foxes and hares abound, and can often be glimpsed in the beams of car headlights at night. Hedgehogs are common: the species in Cyprus has long ears and is a colonist from North Africa.

The reptiles generally hibernate during the cold season, but are much in evidence once the warmer weather arrives. Outside, snakes glide past, escaping into the long grass, or a nook in the garden wall. The black ones, which are the most common, are quite harmless. However the sandy coloured blunt-nosed viper is highly poisonous, and will not flee when approached. Lizards and dragon lizards bask in the sun, and scamper off into clefts in the dry-stone walls when disturbed. The observant visitor will notice the odd chameleon mimicking the greenery as it clambers in slow motion, gripping the plant stems carefully with its mittened feet, eyes swivelling watchfully in their turrets. Inside, pink geckos may be seen and heard, as they scuttle up the walls in search of a snack.

Sea turtles visit the more isolated northern beaches during the summer to lay their eggs in holes scooped out of the sand. The preferred sites are to the east of Kyrenia, towards the Karpas, but visitors should take care not to disturb them.

GENERAL INFORMATION

Access to Northern Cyprus

As Northern Cyprus remains unrecognized by most of the international community, there are no direct flights from Europe. However, some charter companies avoid this problem by touching down in Turkey before proceeding to Ercan, the airport located a few miles to the east of Nicosia. In addition, there are regular flights by Cyprus Turkish Airlines and Turkish Airlines between Ercan and all the major airports in Turkey, which are linked by the international carriers to most destinations in Europe.

There are also regular car-ferry services between Famagusta and Mersin (Turkey), and Kyrenia and Taşucu (Turkey). It is possible to drive from London to Cyprus in four days, or travel with one of the several bus services which operate between England and North Cyprus, but this can be an exhausting and sometimes harrowing way to start a holiday. For non package-tour visitors, the addresses below of two airlines which fly to Northern Cyprus may be useful.

Cyprus Turkish Airlines:

> 41, Pall Mall St. London SW1
> Tel: 71 930 4851

Turkish Airlines:

> 11, Hanover St. London
> Tel: 71 499 9240

Travel Documents

A valid passport is required for visitors to Northern Cyprus. To avoid problems on subsequent visits to Greece, or Southern Cyprus, the immigration officer will, on request, stamp the visitor's visa on a separate sheet of paper, instead of directly in the passport.

It should be pointed out that visitors arriving through ports of entry in Northern Cyprus can under no circumstances visit Southern Cyprus. Tourists in Southern Cyprus can usually obtain permission for a day trip to the north.

Information

Below are the addresses of the Turkish Cypriot representative in London, and the British High Commission Annexe in Nicosia:

Turkish Cypriot Office: 28, Cockspur St., London SW1 Y5BN
Tel.: 071 839 4577

British High Commission: Mehmet Akif Caddesi, Nicosia
Tel.: 020 71938 / 83861

Accommodation

In addition to the regular hotels, self catering bungalows are also available, and are worth considering, particularly for those with children. Before agreeing terms, be sure to check that the facilities offered are in working order. In particular, ensure that the bathroom functions properly, and that fans, air-conditioners (essential in summer), and any other apparatus actually works. Mosquitos can be irritating in the summertime, so rooms fitted with fly-screens are a boon. Mosquito coils (which smoulder when ignited, yielding smoke which mosquitos - and some humans - dislike) can be purchased locally, but it is a good idea to bring some insect repellent with you.

Descriptive lists of hotels and bungalows may be obtained from any of the tourist offices.

Transport

Busses, minibusses, and service taxis (dolmuş) ply the routes between all the towns and many of the larger villages. Regular taxis are also available. Busfares are cheap, and taxis are very reasonable. Whilst public transport will enable the visitor to enjoy 'rubbing shoulders' with the locals, those with limited time are advised to hire a car. The prices are affordable to those used to European rates - in the region of twelve pounds a day during the prime season, and less at other times. An international driving licence, or a national licence valid in the motorist's home country is required. Cypriots drive on the left hand side of the road, as in England. However, there are many left hand drive cars to be seen, which are imported from Turkey. Less experienced drivers are urged to select a right-hand-drive vehicle from the hire car company. Visitors are alerted to the 'free field' style of driving commonly encountered in Cyprus. Note that petrol stations are not ubiquitous: if you anticipate exploring more remote areas, ensure that you tank up first.

140

There are numerous car-hire companies to choose from: a few (in Kyrenia) are listed below. Phone around for the best deal, and check that the hand-brake, indicators, lights etc. function, before you drive away.

Atlantic Car Hire: Dome Hotel   Tel: 53053

Oscar Car Hire: Kordonboyu C.   Tel: 52272

Sun RentaCar: Kordonboyu C.   Tel: 54979

Derv's Car Hire: Ecevit C.   Tel: 54276

Currency

The local curency is the Turkish Lira (TL), but Cyprus pounds, sterling, deutschmarks, and US dollars may often be used directly. Major credit cards are accepted in some shops and hotels. Cash and travellers cheques may be changed in banks, but the visitor may find a more favourable rate at the moneychangers. It is recommended that small amounts are changed as required, as hard currencies tend to rise against the TL as time goes by.

Tourist Information Offices

Information and maps may be obtained from any of the following offices:

Famagusta:	5, Fevzi Çakmak Bulvari.	Tel.: 036 - 62864
Ercan Airport:	Terminal Building.	Tel.: 023 - 14737
Kyrenia:	30, Kordonboyu (Old Harbour)	Tel.: 081 - 52145
Nicosia:	95, Mehmet Akif Caddesi.	Tel.: 020 - 75051/2/3

Public Holidays

January 1st	New Years Day
April 23rd	Childrens Day
May 1st	Labour Day
May 19th	Youth and Sports Day
July 20th	Day of Peace & Freedom (Anniversary of the Turkish Intervention)
August 1st	Day of Communal Resistance
August 30th	Victory Day
October 23rd	Prophet Mohammed's Birthday
November 15th	Independence Day (of the T.R.N.C.)

In addition, there are several religious holidays. The dates on which these occur vary, as they are related to the month of fasting, *Ramazan*, which is calculated according to the Lunar calendar.

Şeker Bayram, or the Sugar Festival, takes place at the end of Ramazan, and continues for three days.

Kurban Bayram occurs two months after the Şeker Bayram, and lasts for four days

Museum Opening Times

May to September:	9.00am	- 1.30pm
	4.00pm	- 6.30pm
October to April:	8.00am	- 1.00pm
	2.30pm	- 5.00pm

At the weekends, the following museums are closed: Kumarcılar Han, Büyük Han, Mevlevi Tekke, Bedestan, Lapidary Museum, (all in Nicosia) Othello's Tower, and Canbulat Museum, (both in Famagusta).

Post and Telephone

All mail to North Cyprus should include 'Mersin 10, Turkey' in the address instead of 'North Cyprus', otherwise it is quite likely to end up in the southern sector of Cyprus, which is inaccessible to tourists arriving in the north.

Post office hours: Weekdays: 8am - 1pm; 2pm - 5pm
Saturdays: 9am - 12 noon. Closed on Sunday

Public telephone boxes are not common, and visitors will usually phone from their hotel, or from the Telecommunications Office, which in Kyrenia is opposite the Post Office.

The telephone codes for North Cyprus are listed below:

North Cyprus	(00)905	For example, to call the Kyrenia number
Kyrenia	(0)81	54321 from England, dial 010 905 81 54321
Nicosia	(0)20	
Famagusta	(0)36	

Most European countries may be dialled directly from North Cyprus. The code for England is 0044. Codes for other countries are listed in the telephone directory. For example, to call the London number 081 765 4321, dial 0044 81 765 4321.

Climate

Spring and Autumn are the most pleasant seasons in Cyprus. The days are generally warm and sunny, but without the enervating heat of mid-summer. Visitors should include a pullover and/or a lightweight jacket in their travel wardrobe for strolls in the cool of the evening, or when dining at the open-air restaurants. The winter months are by no means to be avoided: the air is fresh, and the skies are often clear and sunny. However, the evenings can be chilly, and of course the days are shorter. Warmer clothes are obviously called for.

Average water and air temperatures (°C)

Month	Water	Air	Month	Water	Air
January	16	14	*July*	26	29
February	17	14	*August*	28	29
March	17	15	*September*	27	25
April	19	18	*October*	25	25
May	21	21	*November*	22	18
June	24	24	*December*	19	13

This is certainly not true for the summer months: during July and August, visitors will need only the lightest and loosest clothing. The sun can be very strong, and care should be taken to avoid sunburn, by progressive exposure to the sun, and the use of sun-screen lotions.

Temperatures in the interior of the island tend to be more extreme than those in the coastal areas, which are moderated by the sea, and off-shore breezes.

Beaches

Beaches are a principal attraction in North Cyprus, and vary widely in character from the busy hotel beaches, which offer many facilities, to the secluded stretches of sand in the Karpas, where the visitor may have an entire beach to himself. Some of the beaches are unfortunately spoilt by accumulations of garbage: visitors are urged to take their rubbish away with them. A tip: tar may be removed from clothes or the skin by rubbing gently with olive oil. Take a small bottle with you to the beach. Do not forget to use sun-screen lotion - after 20 minutes under the summer sun, you will begin to burn.

Watersports are available on some beaches, in particular at Deniz Kızı, some 5 miles west of Kyrenia, where Dolphin Sailing, which is recognized by the Royal Yacht Club, offers a wide range of watersports with professional tuition and supervision. In general, the beaches associated with hotels are kept clean, and provide facilities such as toilets, deck chairs, parasols, bars and restaurants. Entrance fees vary. The visitor is encouraged to explore for himself, but as a guide, a few beaches are listed below.

Acapulco Beach lies about 6 miles to the east of Kyrenia. At the point where the coast road to the east sweeps up towards the mountains, a large sign advertising this beach will be seen. Here the road branches off to the left, passing through an army camp before leading to the entrance of this holiday complex. This is a popular tourist beach, offering most facilities, but supervision of children swimming is recommended as there is an undertow. Windsurfing is available.

Lara Beach may be found a couple of miles further on - a sign indicates where to turn off from the new by-pass road. Toilets, showers, and beach chairs are available, and there is also a reasonable open air restaurant.

Alakadı Beach is still further east, about 10 miles from Kyrenia. A hundred yards or so past St. Kathleen's restaurant is a small bridge. Immediately after the bridge, a rough track bears left, leading past a farm and through the dunes to a large, sweeping double bay. There are no facilities, so bring your own refreshments, including water, and avoid leaving litter.

Sunset Beach is located about 5 miles to the west of Kyrenia, past the sloping concrete monument beyond Karaoğlanoğlu. It is adjacent to the Altınkaya fish restaurant. The sandy beach is well protected and ideal for tiny tots. Toilets and showers are available, and there is a bar and restaurant.

Deniz Kızı is situated about seven miles west of Kyrenia. This sheltered bay is kept clean, and offers a variety of water sports (see Dolphin Sailing above) including windsurfing, parascending, water skiing, and inflateable fun rafts for smaller children. Deck chairs are available for hire, and there are also toilet and shower facilities.

Mare Monte hotel beach lies some 10 miles west of Kyrenia, and provides all the facilities the visitor requires. An excellent location, but the entrance fee is higher than elsewhere.

The *Dome Hotel* in Kyrenia has a large sea-water swimming pool, ideal for those who like sea-water without the sand. Most facilities available.

Golf

At Yeşilyurt (Pendayia) about 30 miles west of Kyrenia, there is a seven hole golf course. It is open on Tuesdays, Thursdays, and Sundays, but other arrangements are possible. Contact the course keeper, Mr. Ian Cooper for further information. Tel.; 077 17421.

Restaurants

There is an abundance of restaurants in North Cyprus, offering both local and foreign dishes. Characteristic of the local menu is the *meze*. This consists of a dozen or more small dishes containing a variety of cold food, such as beans, beetroot, yoghurt, fishballs, *humus*, etc. from which the diner serves himself. Bread or toast is also provided, and the meze is supplemented at intervals with freshly cooked items, such as fried *hellim* cheese, or a plate of deep fried *kalamari* (squid). The meze is followed by the main course, which is usually accompanied by chips and a salad. Fish or *kebab* (meat chunks roasted on skewers) are popular choices for the main course, but chicken is also available in some places. The meal ends with fruit, followed by Turkish coffee and local cognac. The coffee is served *sade* (no sugar), *orta* (some sugar), or *şekerli* (sweet).

(From the Metin Münir collection)

The diner will enjoy many excellent meals in North Cyprus. However, the quality and service in many of the restaurants is very variable. There are a few exceptions: for a reliable meze followed by fish, try the *Altınkaya* restaurant, located about 5 miles west of Kyrenia, just past the sloping concrete monument, on the right. There is a sign, but it is easy to miss at night. Plenty of space for children to run about, and there are swings outside. Further west, shortly before Deniz Kızı, the *St. Tropez* is a new restaurant specializing in French-style cuisine. Next door to the Celebrity, further west, the *Marmaris* offers excellent meze and fish. For European style food, the *Grapevine* in Kyrenia (next to the Esso petrol station on the road to Nicosia, as you leave Kyrenia) is highly recommended. A popular haunt of the expatriates, who are drawn by the pleasant ambience and the low bar prices. Open lunch times and evenings, except Sundays. Just around the corner, *Effendi's* is usually packed. Another reliable restaurant in Kyrenia, past the Dome Hotel, on the left, is *Niyazi's Restaurant.* A good selection of Turkish Cypriot cuisine is offered here, including meze, and kebab. The *Harbour Club* situated towards the castle end of Kyrenia harbour is well appointed, and offers a select European menu. Located a couple of miles to the east of Kyrenia at Karakum, the *Courtyard* is a popular pub and restaurant. *Abbey House*, situated on the east side of Bellapais Abbey, is a restaurant serving excellent European style food, and offering a wide choice of wines. It is open in the evenings, except Sundays.

The selection above in no way condemns the restaurants not mentioned: the setting of a meal is often as important as the food itself, and many visitors delight in dining in one of the many restaurants overlooking Kyrenia harbour, or up in the hills at Karmi. The more adventurous should also try the *lokantas*, where they will find that the local dishes are both excellent and cheap.

No instruction is necessary regarding the wines and beer (lager only), which may accompany the meal - the visitor will quickly learn which are to his taste. However, two drinks not common in Europe should be sampled: *rakı*, a spirit derived from aniseed, is widely consumed, often as an aperitif. This clear liquor turns milky, when diluted with water. Regarded by many as the national drink, the *brandy-sour* enrols many fans amongst those seeking a long drink during the hot weather. It is concocted from brandy, bitters, lemon, and soda water. A most refreshing non-alcoholic drink is *ayran*, made from yoghurt, water, salt, and a sprinkling of chopped mint leaves

BIBLIOGRAPHY

Cobham C.D. Excerpta Cypria: Materials for a History of Cyprus
Cambridge 1908.

Dikaios P. Khirokitia, Oxford, 1953

Dreghorn W. A Guide to the Antiquities of Kyrenia, Nicosia, 1977.

Enlart C. L'Art Gothique et la Renaissance en Chypre, 2 vol.,Paris 1899.

Gjerstad E. Ages and Days in Cyprus, Goteborg, 1980.

Gjerstad E. Studies on Prehistoric Cyprus, Uppsala, 1926.

Gunnis R. Historic Cyprus, 1936; 2nd. edition 1947.

Hill G.F.A. A History of Cyprus, 4 vol., Cambridge 1949-52.

Hogarth D.G. Devia Cypria: Archaeological Journey in Cyprus
Oxford: Frowde 1889

Jeffery G. Historic Monuments of Cyprus, Nicosia 1918, reprinted 1983.

Karageorghis V. Cyprus ('Archeologia Mundi' series), 1968

Karageorghis V. Salamis in Cyprus, 1969

Karageorghis V. The Civilization of Prehistoric Cyprus, 1976.

Luke, Sir Harry Cyprus, A Portrait and Appreciation, London, 1957

Newman P. A Short History of Cyprus, London 1940.

Runciman S. A History of the Crusades, 3 vol., Cambridge, 1951-54.

Salvator Archduke Louis Levkosia, the Capital of Cyprus, repr.1983.

Spyridakis C. A Brief History of Cyprus, Nicosia, 1964.

Stylianou A.& J. The Painted Churches of Cyprus, London, 1985.

GLOSSARY

Agora: public square or market place.

Ambulatory: aisle around the east end of a church behind the altar.

Apse: semi-circular or polygonal structure terminating the sanctuary at the east end of a church.

Arcade: row of arches resting on columns.

Architrave: (structure) refers to horizontal beams resting on columns.

Ashlar: masonry of squared stones.

Atrium: fore-court of a basilica; court surrounded by columns.

Ayia: Saint (female).

Ayios: Saint (male).

Basilica: architectural form taken over by the Christians for places of worship.

Bema: chancel or sanctuary in Byzantine churches.

Capital: capstone of column.

Cenotaph: symbolic grave.

Clerestory: upper storey of a church, perforated with windows for illuminating the nave.

Corbel: projecting block supporting weight, eg vaulting.

Hypocaust: floor heating of Roman baths.

Iconostasis: screen in front of the sanctuary in an Orthodox church.

Jihad: holy war against unbelievers.

Machicoulis: external gallery supported on corbels with holes in the floor for dropping missiles on the enemy below.

Megaron: main room in a Greek house.

Merlon: upward pointing part of a battlement.

Mihrab: niche in a mosque facing the direction of Mecca.

Mimbar: pulpit in a mosque

Narthex: western sub-division of a church; vestibule, or porch.

Nave: main body of a church, from the narthex to the transept.

Opus Sectile: ornamental surface of different coloured stones.

Orchestra: semi-circular stage in a Greek theatre.

Panayia: the Blessed Virgin Mary

Pantokrator: the Almighty, often depicted in the dome of a church.

Peristyle: columned gangway around a courtyard.

Refectory: dining room, especially in an abbey, or monastery.

Stoa: portico or roofed colonnade.

Synthronon: semi-circle of seats in the main apse, for the clergy.

Tekke: Islamic equivalent of a monastery.

Tholos: a circular building

Tracery: ornamental carved element of Gothic architecture, used to divide a window or arch opening.

Transept: transverse section of a church joining the nave and sanctuary

Triforium: arcaded passage opening onto the nave above the aisle vaulting

Tympanum: flat surface above the lintel and below the arch of a doorway or window.

INDEX

REGISTER OF NAMES

152